T0104356

Conquer the Day

Conquer the Day

A Book of Affirmations

Josh Mecouch

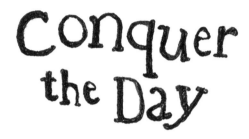

HARPER
DESIGN
An Imprint of HarperCollins Publishers

For information address Harper Design, 195 Broadway, New York, New York 10007. HarperCollins books may be purchased for educational, business, or sales promotional use. For information please email the Special Markets Department at SPsales@harpercollins.com.

Published in 2021 by
Harper Design
An Imprint of
HarperCollins*Publishers*
195 Broadway
New York, NY 10007
Tel: (212) 207-7000
Fax: (855) 746-6023
harperdesign@harpercollins.com
www.hc.com

Distributed throughout the world by
HarperCollins Publishers
195 Broadway
New York, NY 10007

ISBN 978-0-06-301649-1
Library of Congress Control Number LCCN 2020052663
Printed in Malaysia
First Printing, 2021

to
Amber

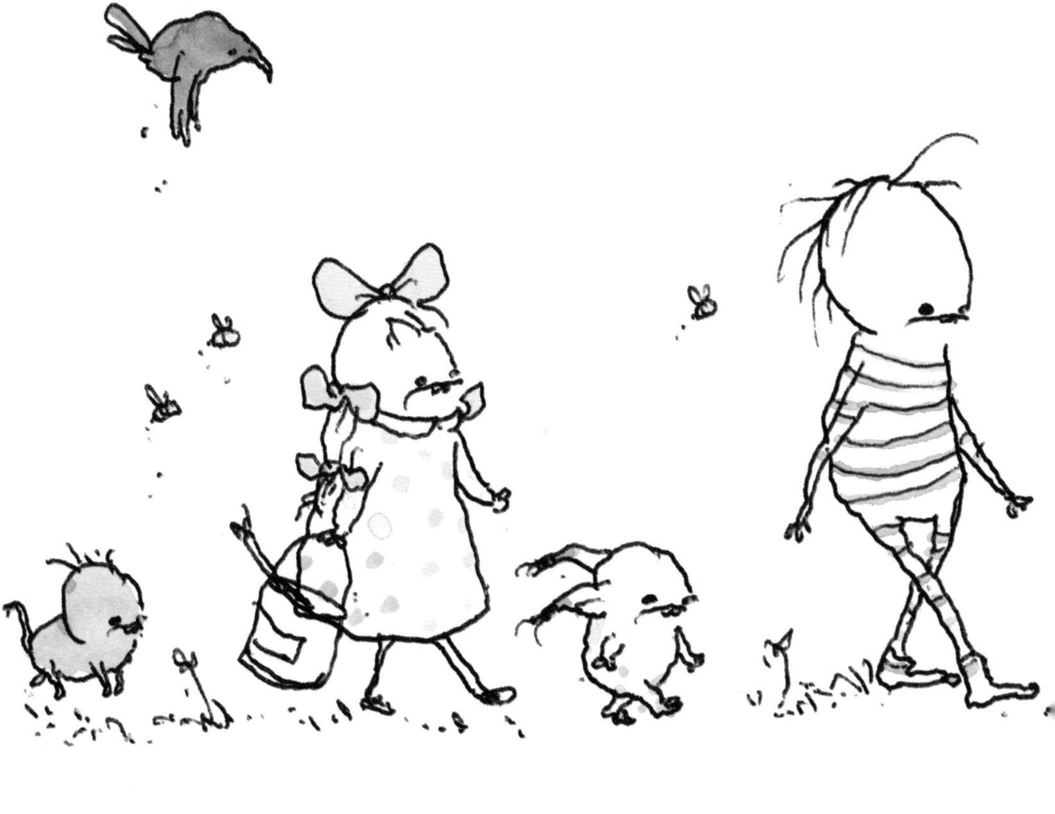

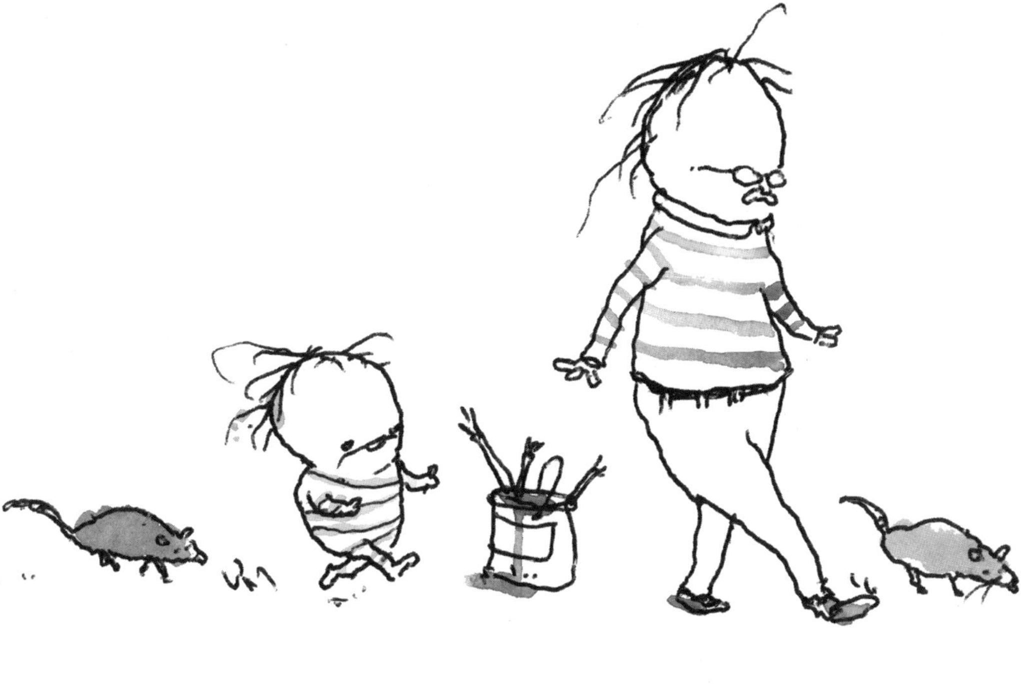

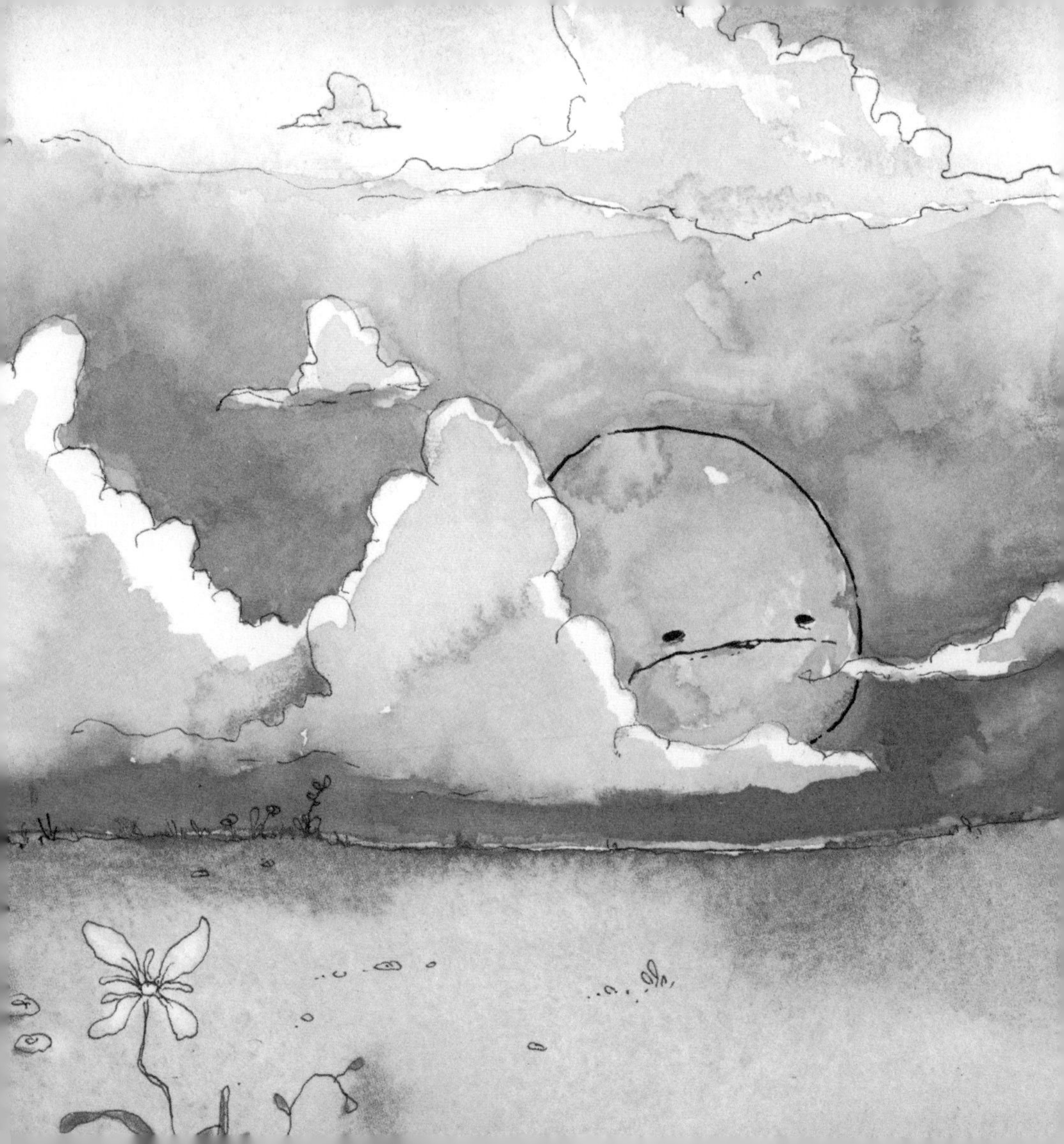

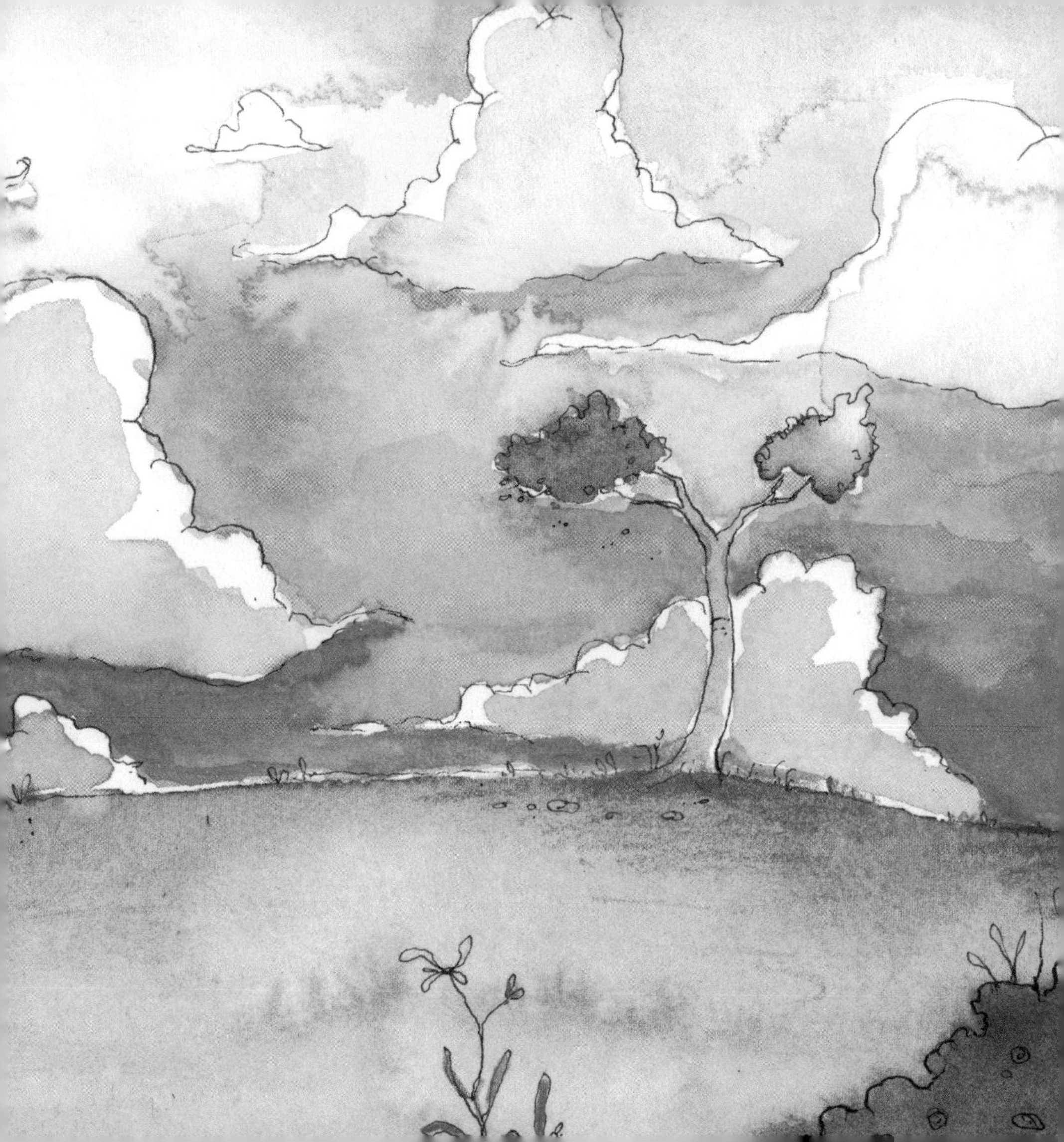

i attack
the day
with energy
and conviction

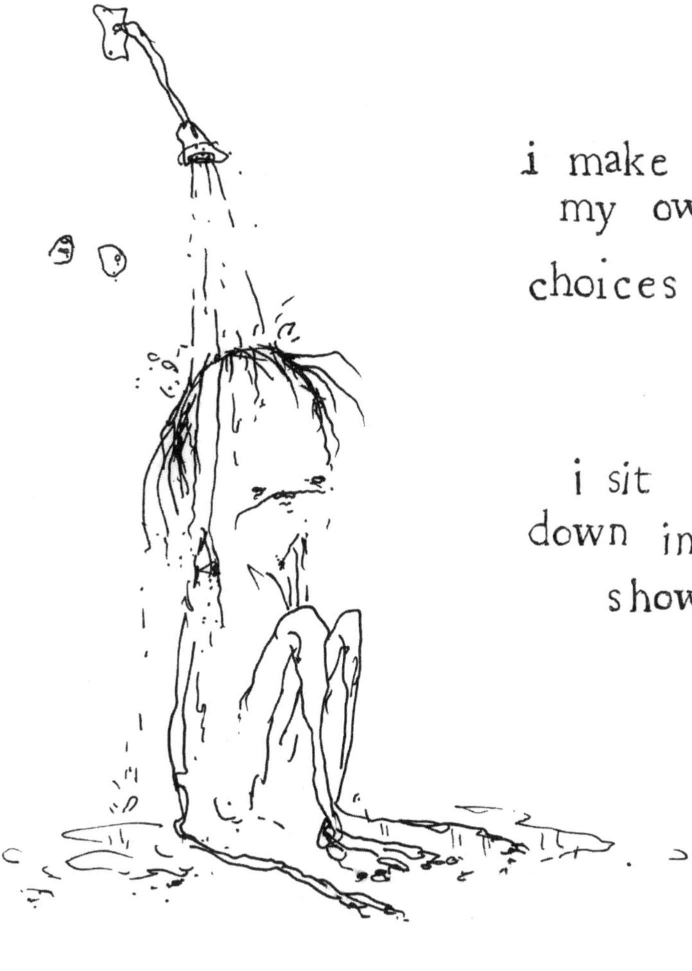

i make
my own
choices

i sit
down in the
shower

discipline is my
second nature

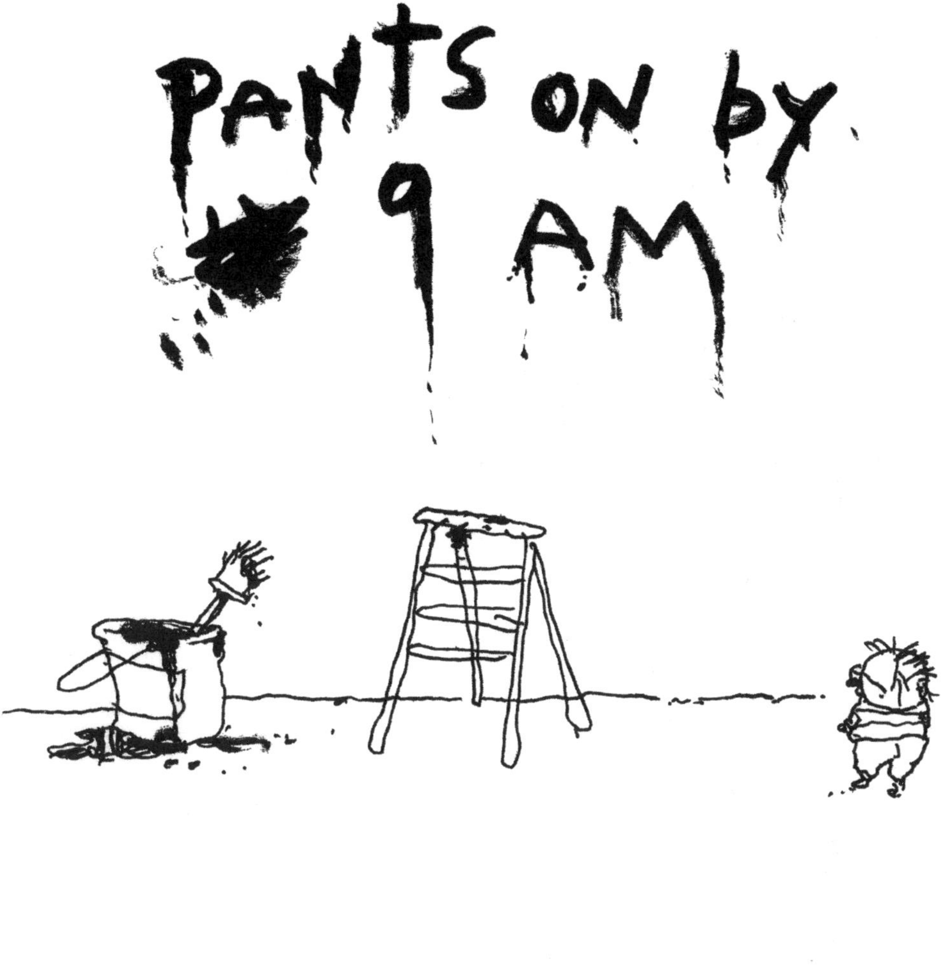
PANTS ON BY
9 AM

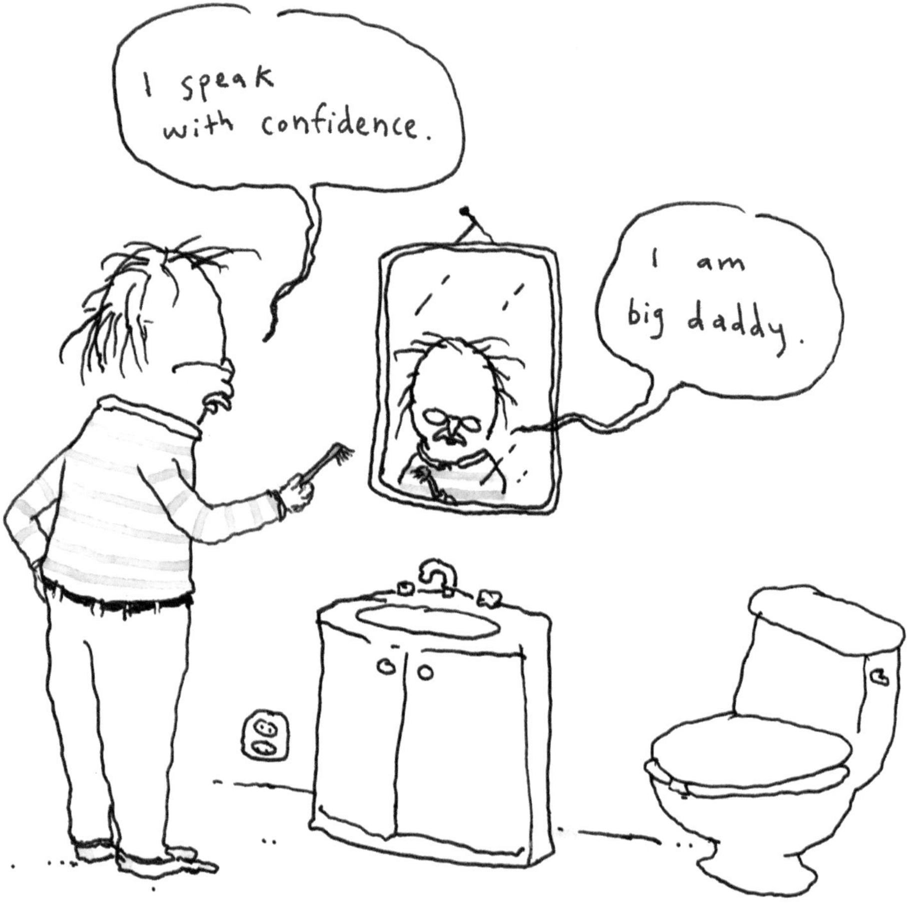
I speak with confidence.
I am big daddy.

my fears are fading away

my path to ~~sucess~~ is inevitable
success

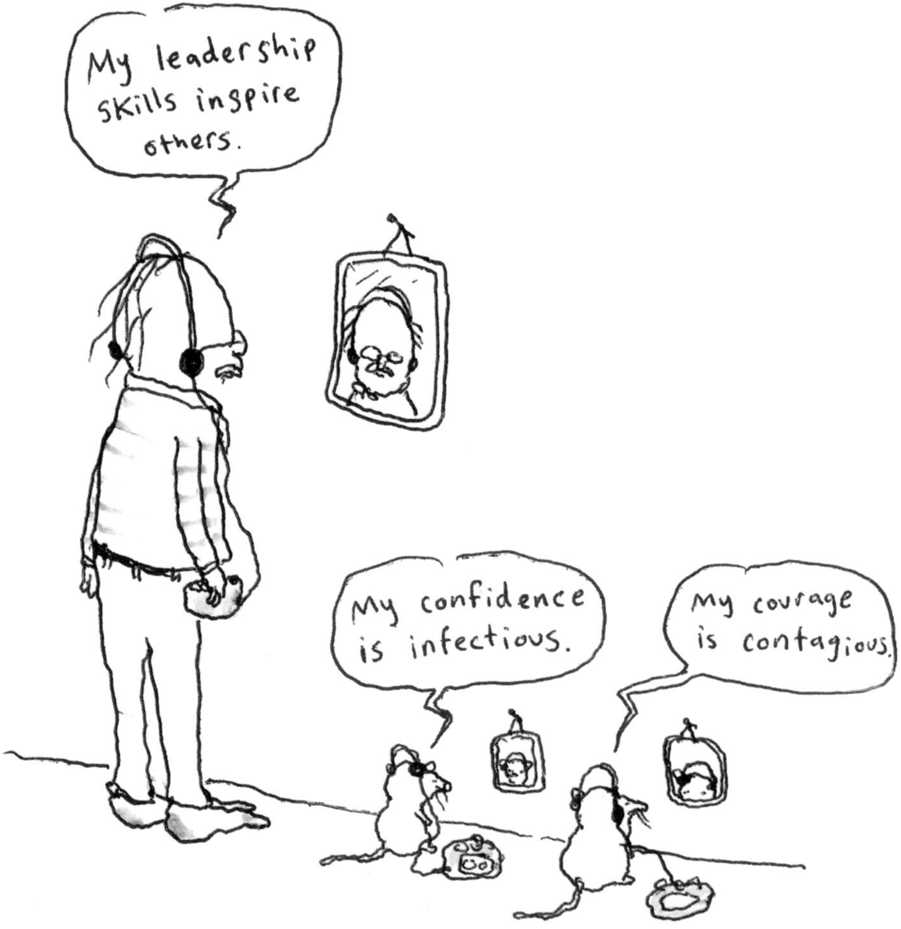
My leadership skills inspire others.
My confidence is infectious.
My courage is contagious.

i am ready
to face new
challenges

my courage
is growing

i live life
on my terms

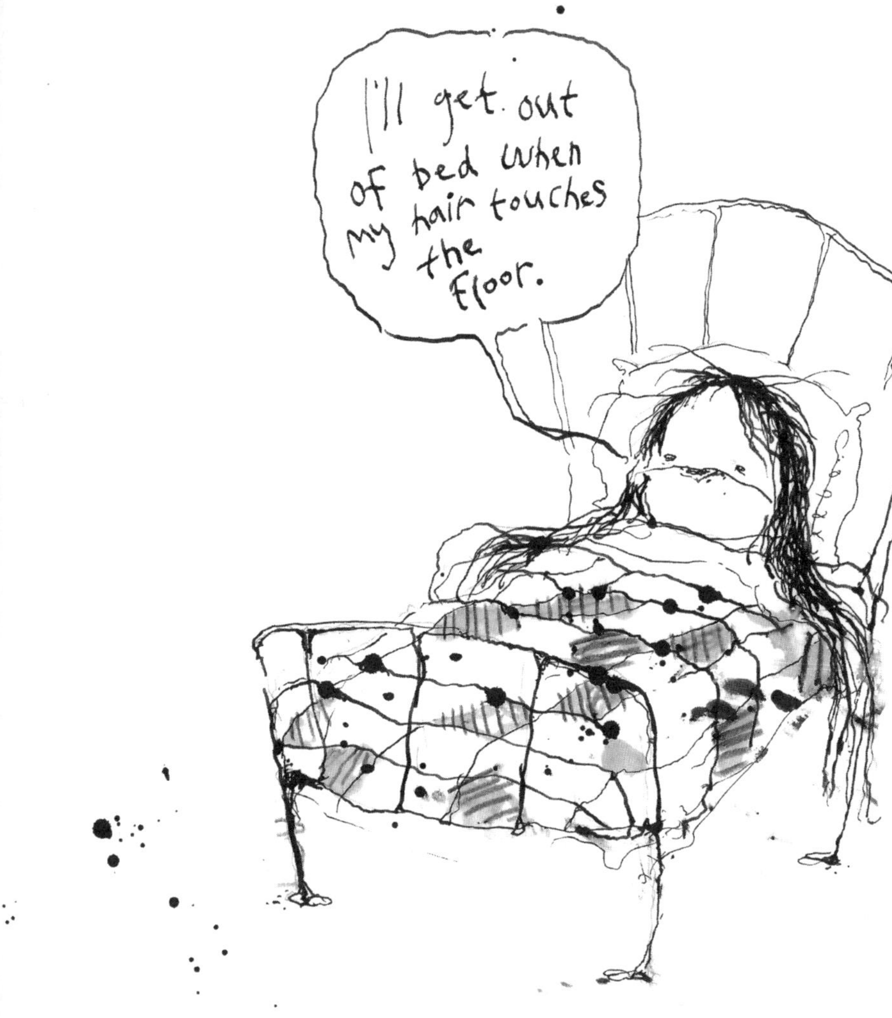
I'll get out of bed when my hair touches the floor.

my self-worth expands with every breath

i inhale confidence and exhale weakness

life is filled with
abundance

others' success
fills me with joy

i take time to help others

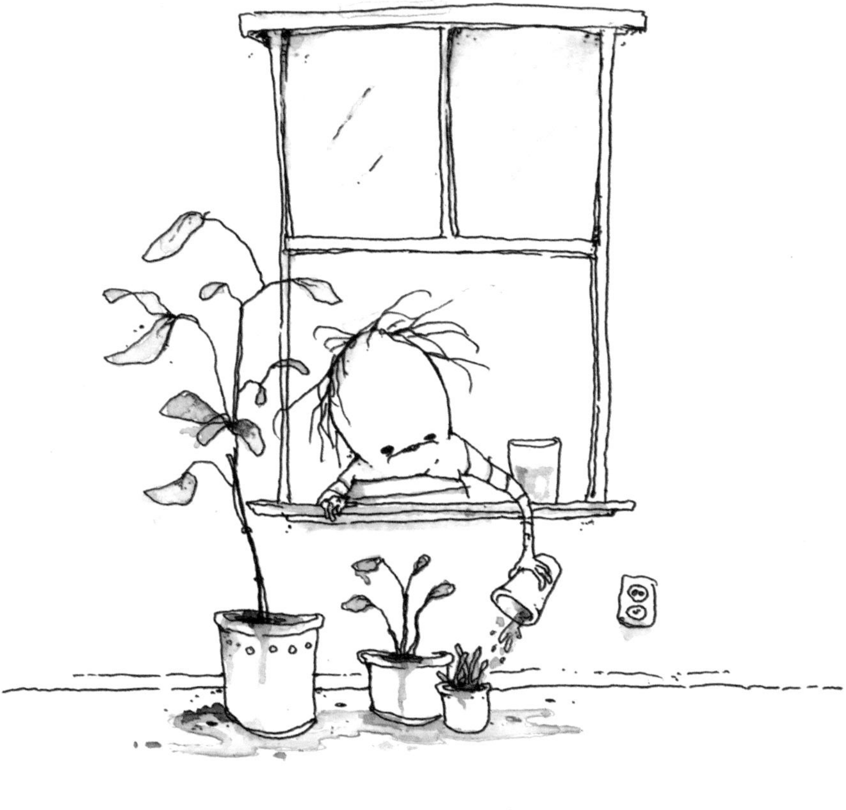

i water strangers' houseplants

i approve of myself
just as i am

my life is full
of meaning

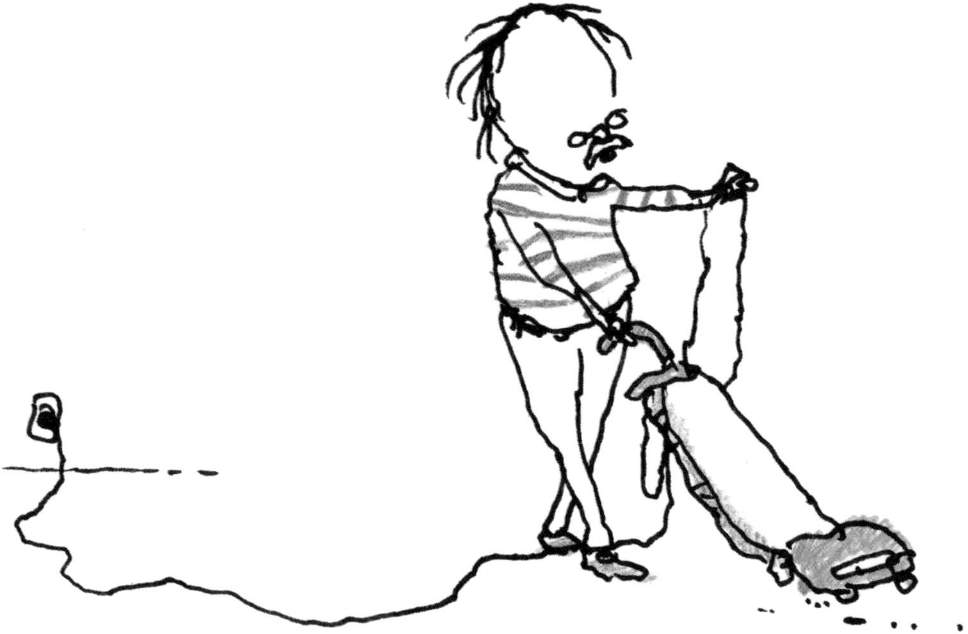

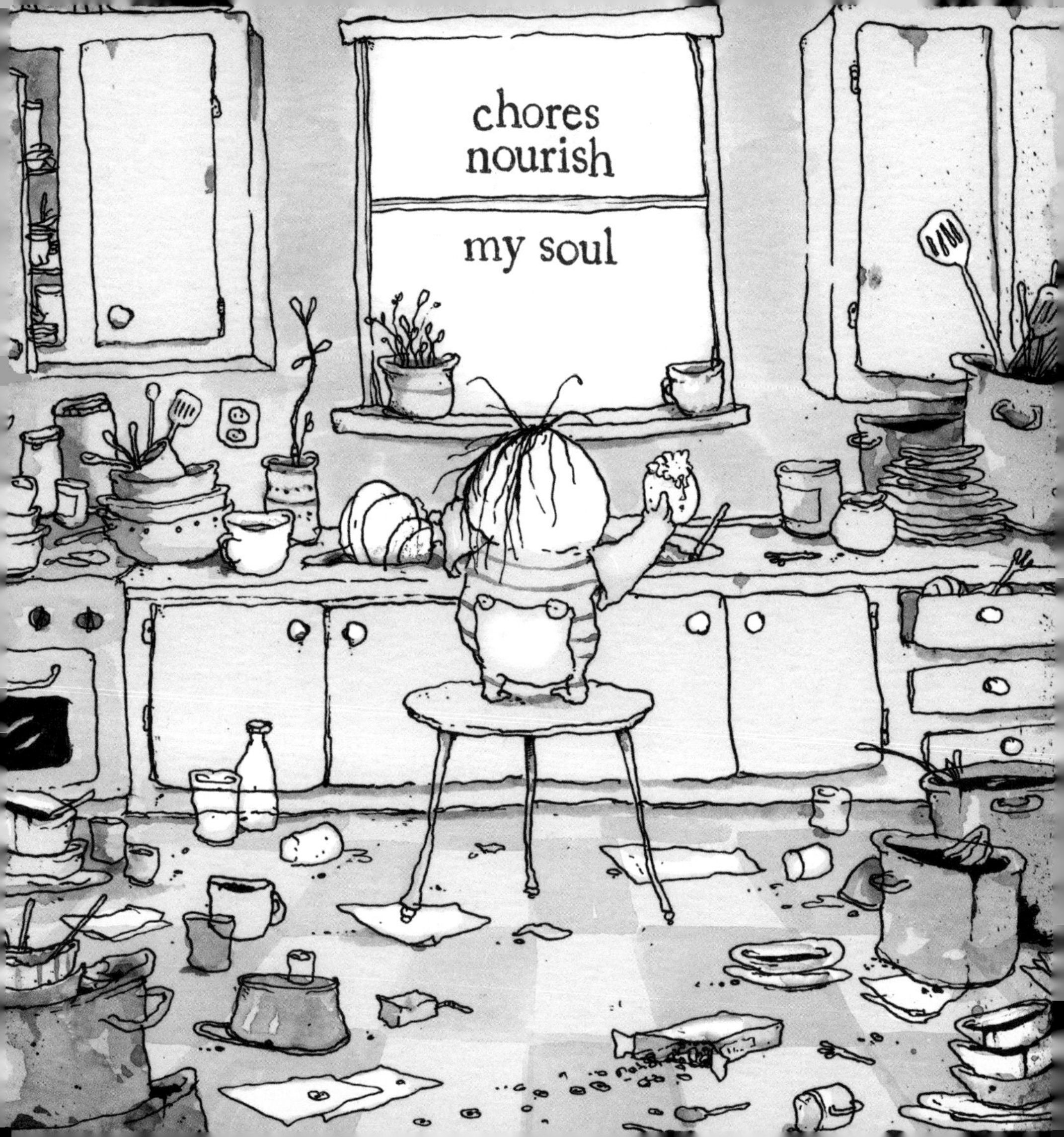
chores
nourish
my soul

i am in touch
with my creative side

i nurture my inner artist

i give my
inner saboteur
 activities to calm
down

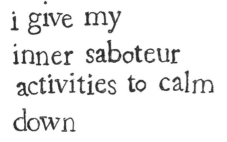

i am in control
of self-sabotage

i tend
to my
own
garden

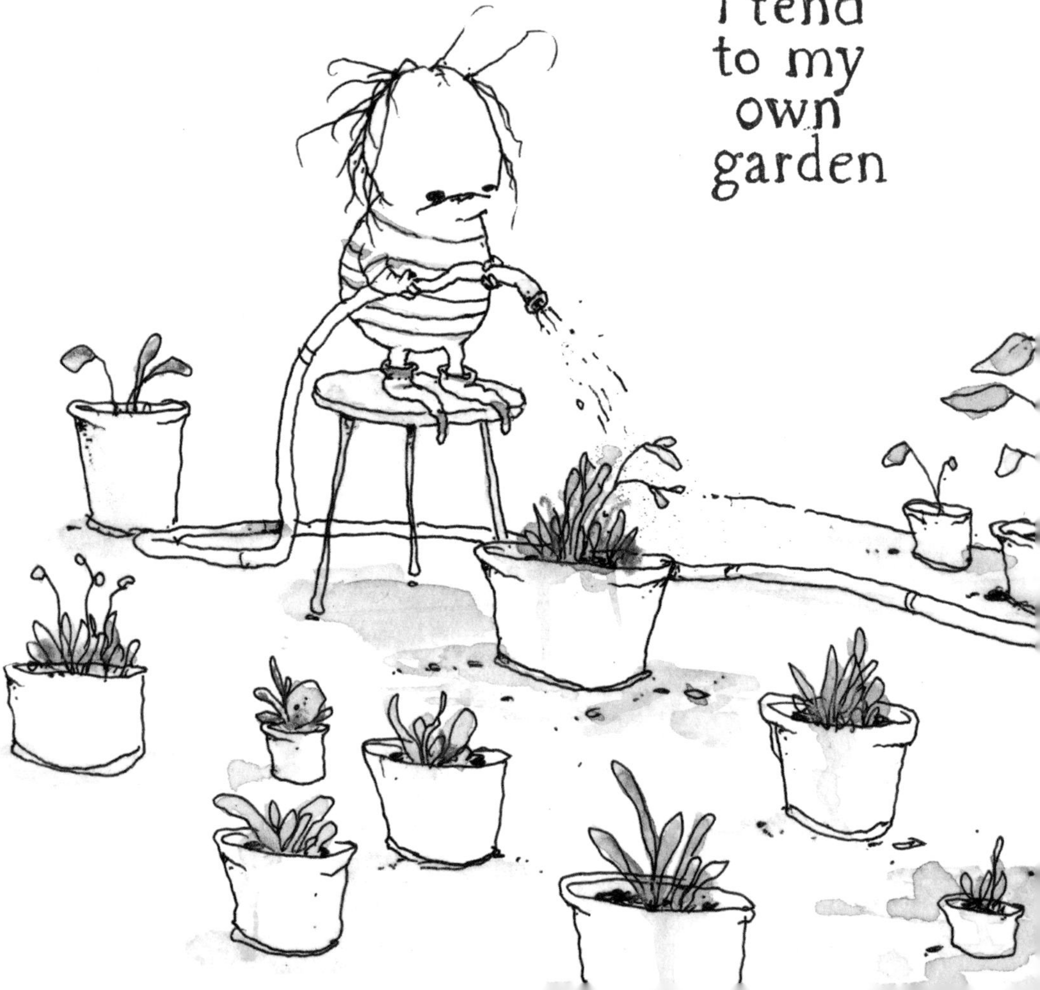

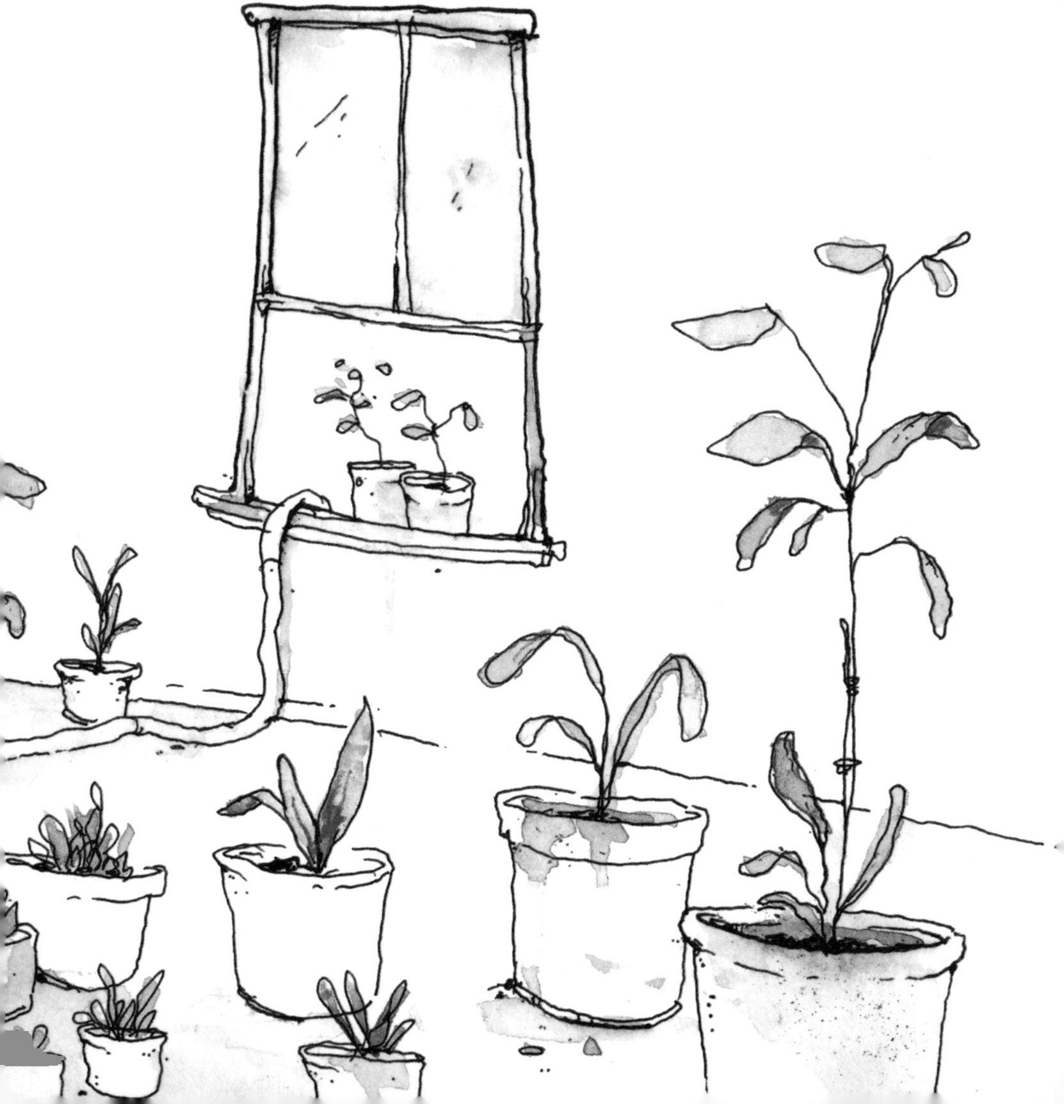

i am taking small
steps towards my
ideal future

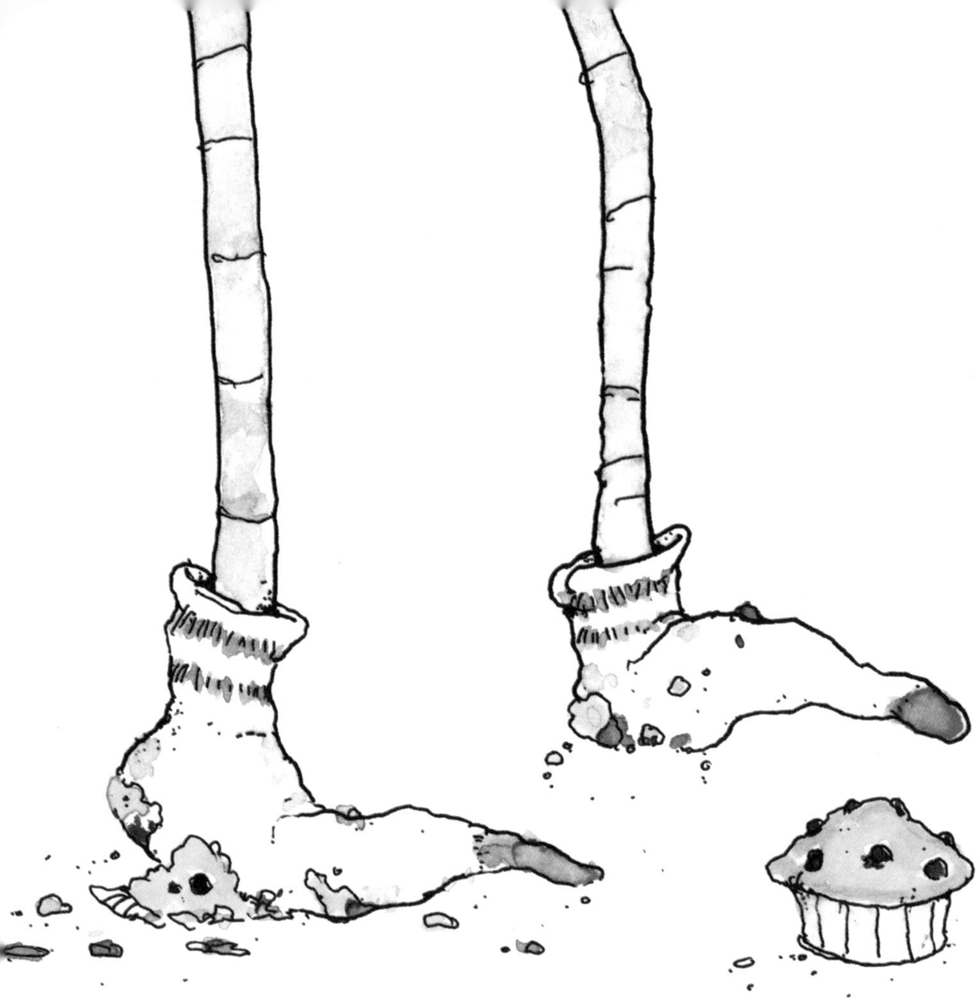

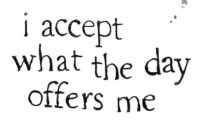

i accept
what the day
offers me

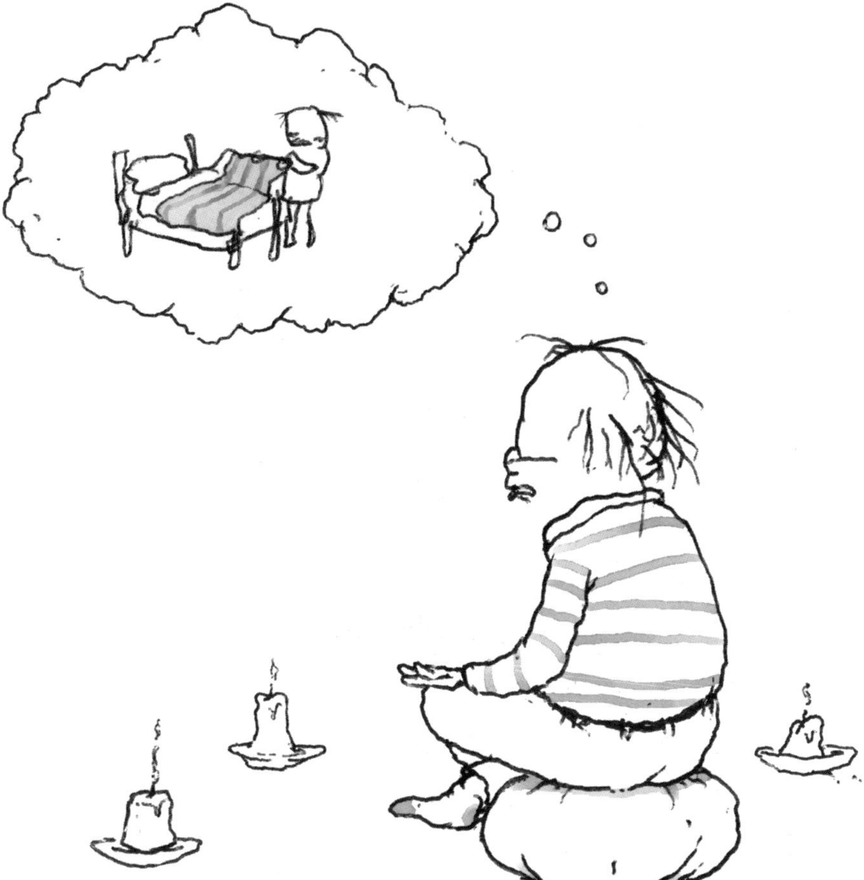

i visualize myself becoming a bed maker

i focus
  on what
i can control

i
organize
my socks

i let go
of what is
unnecessary

i embrace
minimalism

today
i am filled
with energy

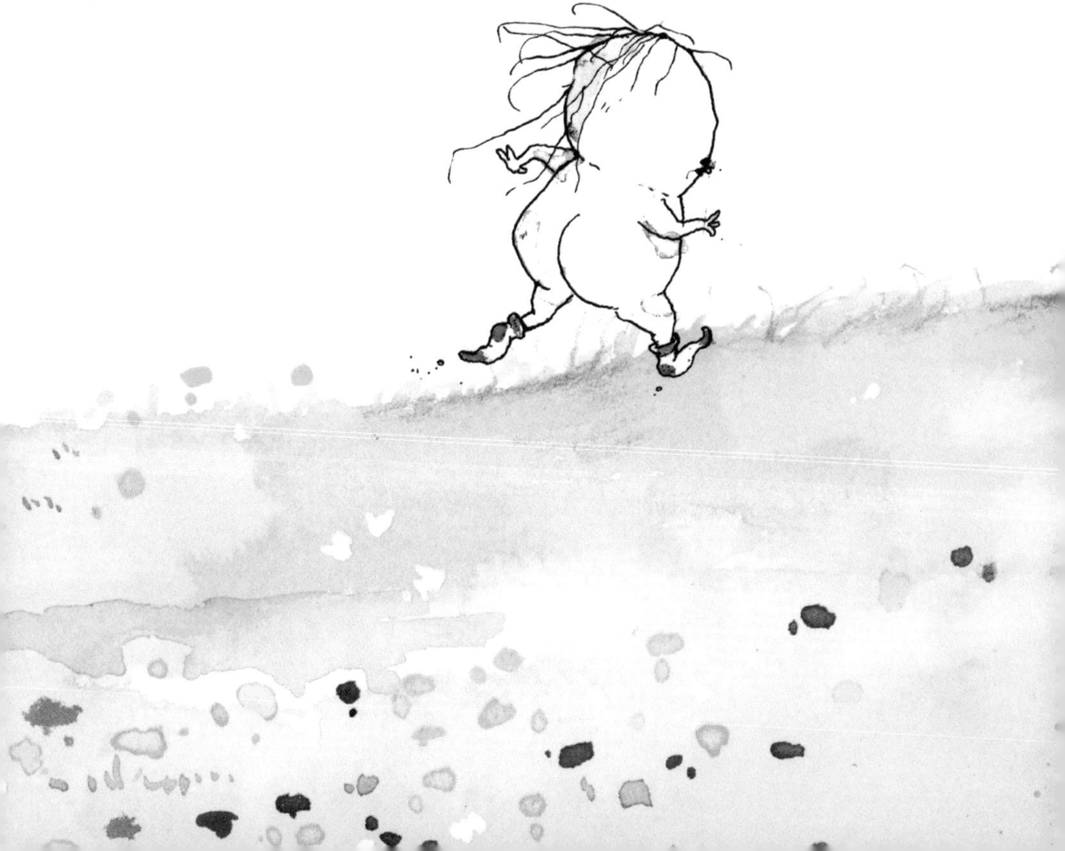

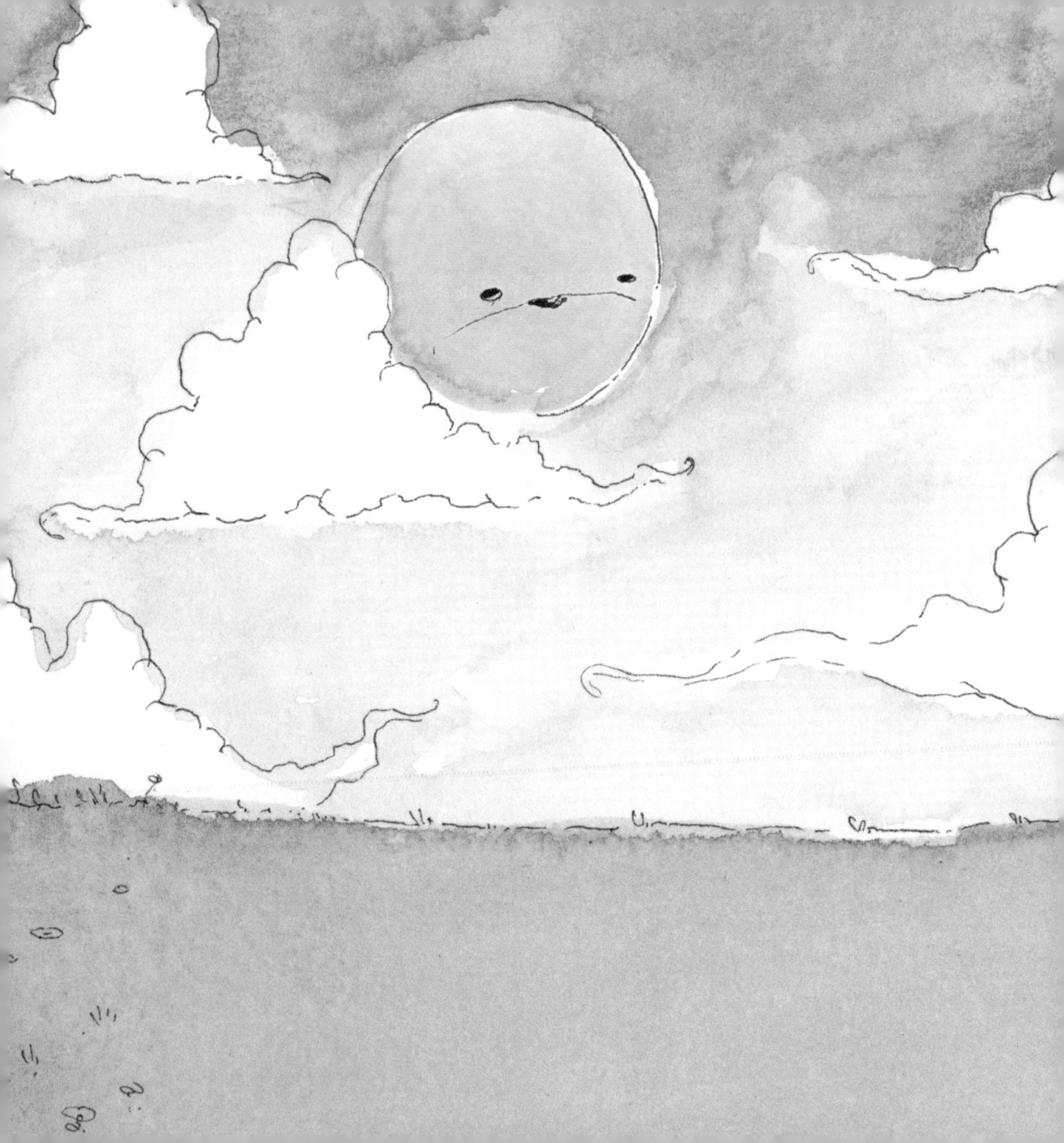

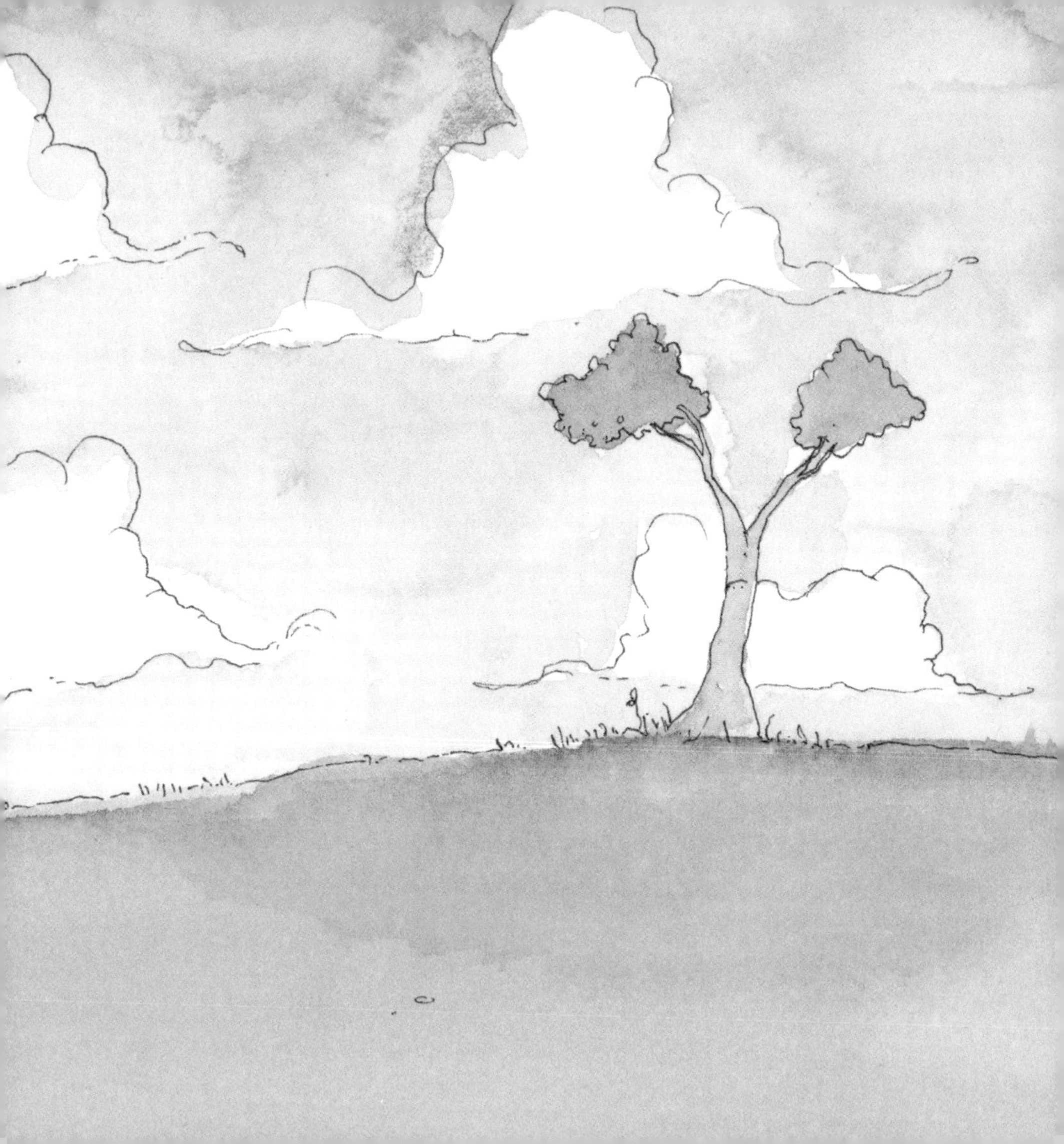

reality obeys
my words

i speak truth
into existence

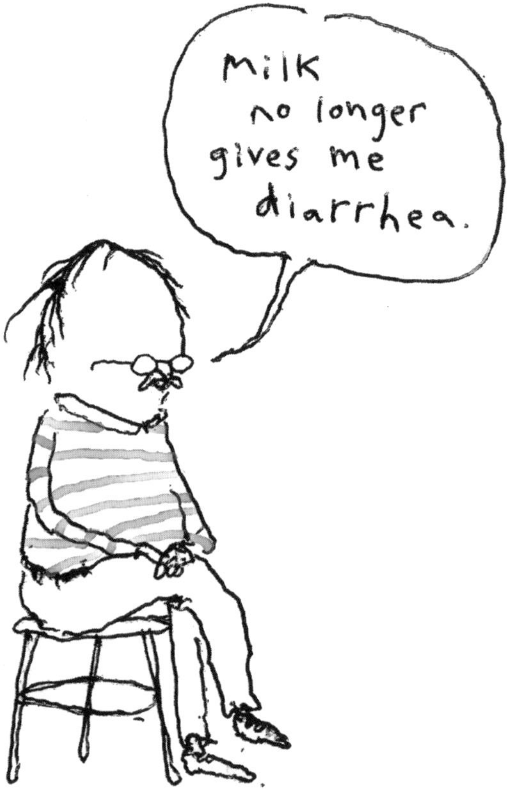
milk no longer gives me diarrhea.

i am willing to take risks

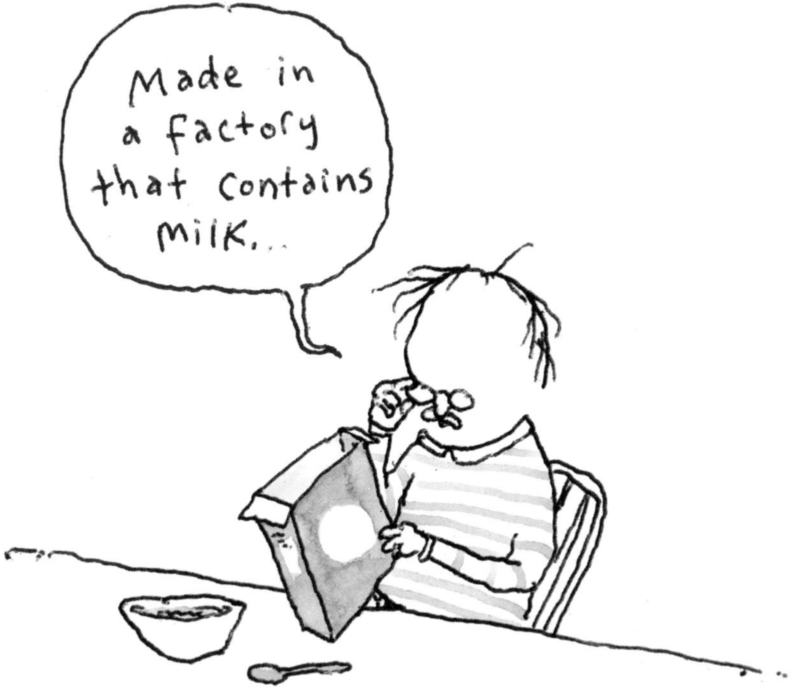
Made in a factory that contains milk...

i fix what
i have broken

i have the tools i need to succeed

i am the architect of my life

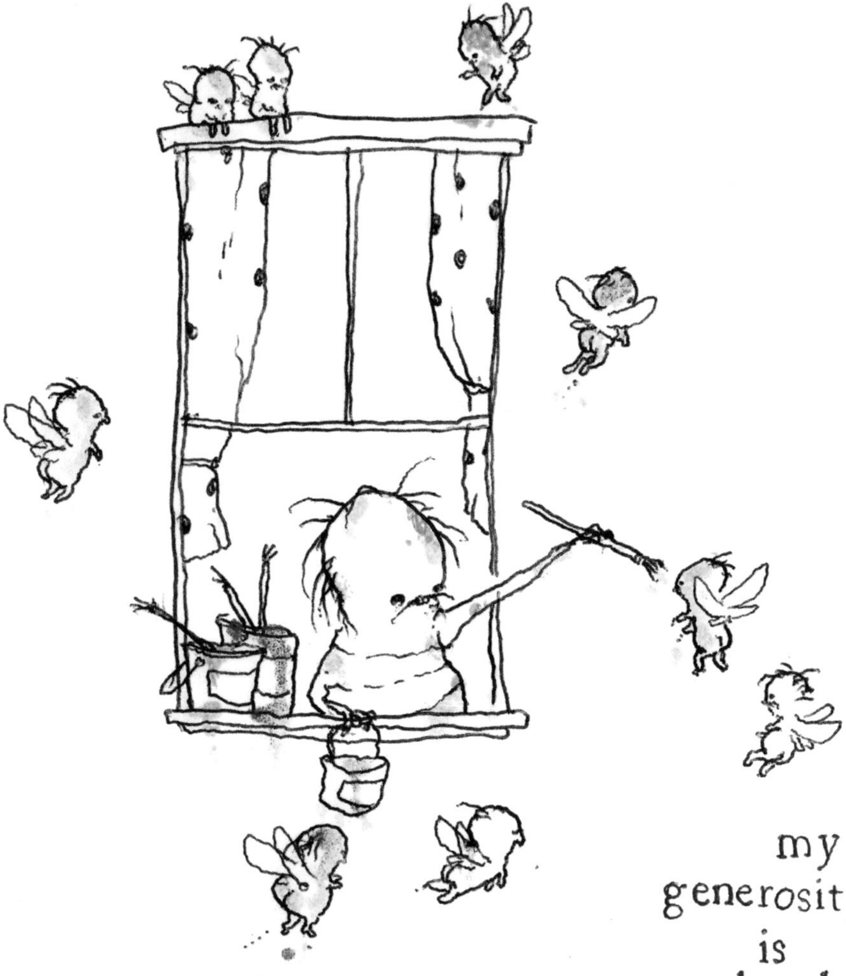

my
generosity
is
relentless

i write down
my goals and
take action

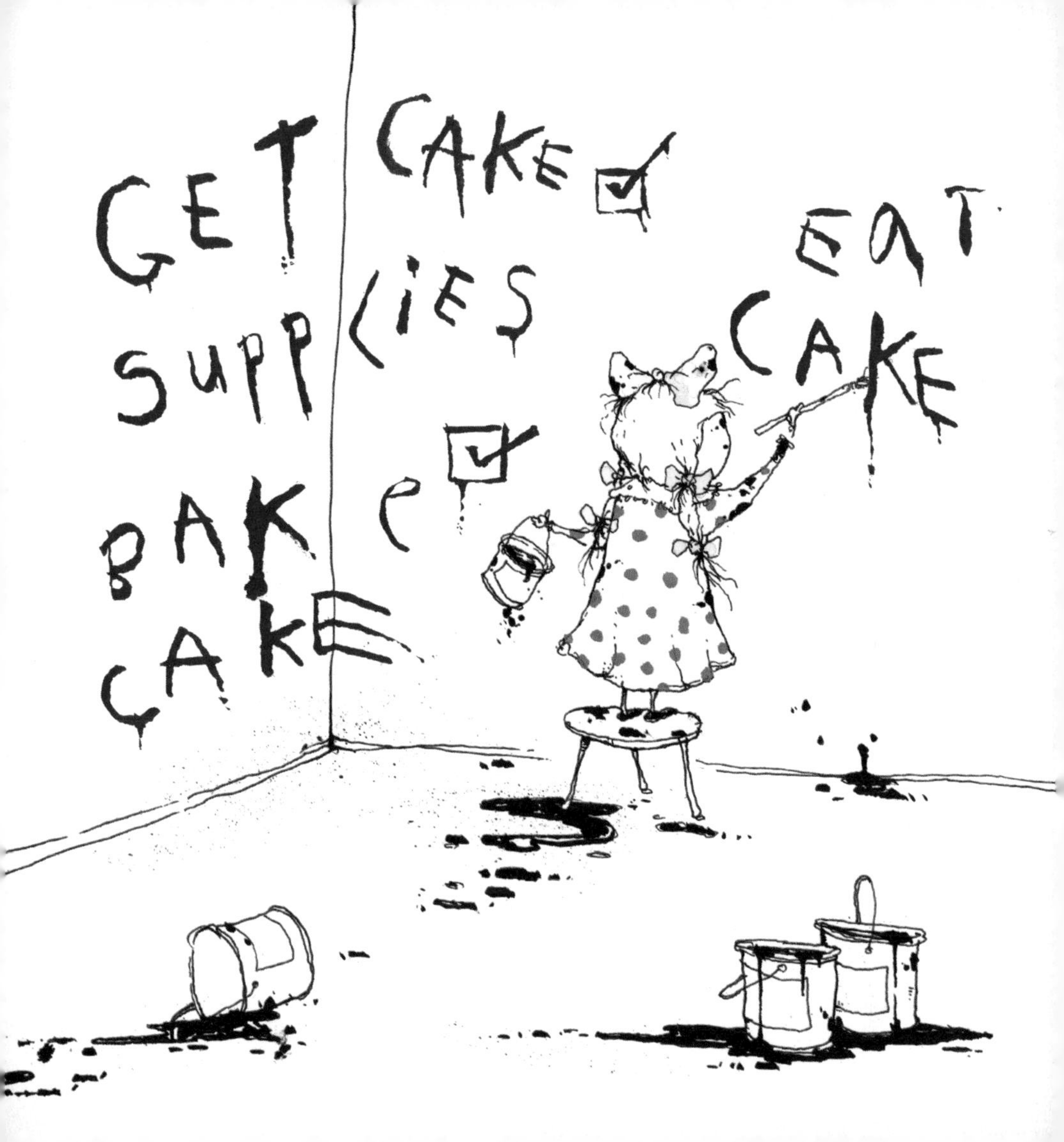
GET CAKE SUPPLIES
BAKE CAKE
EAT CAKE

extreme wealth
is always seeking me

i am open
to receiving this
wealth

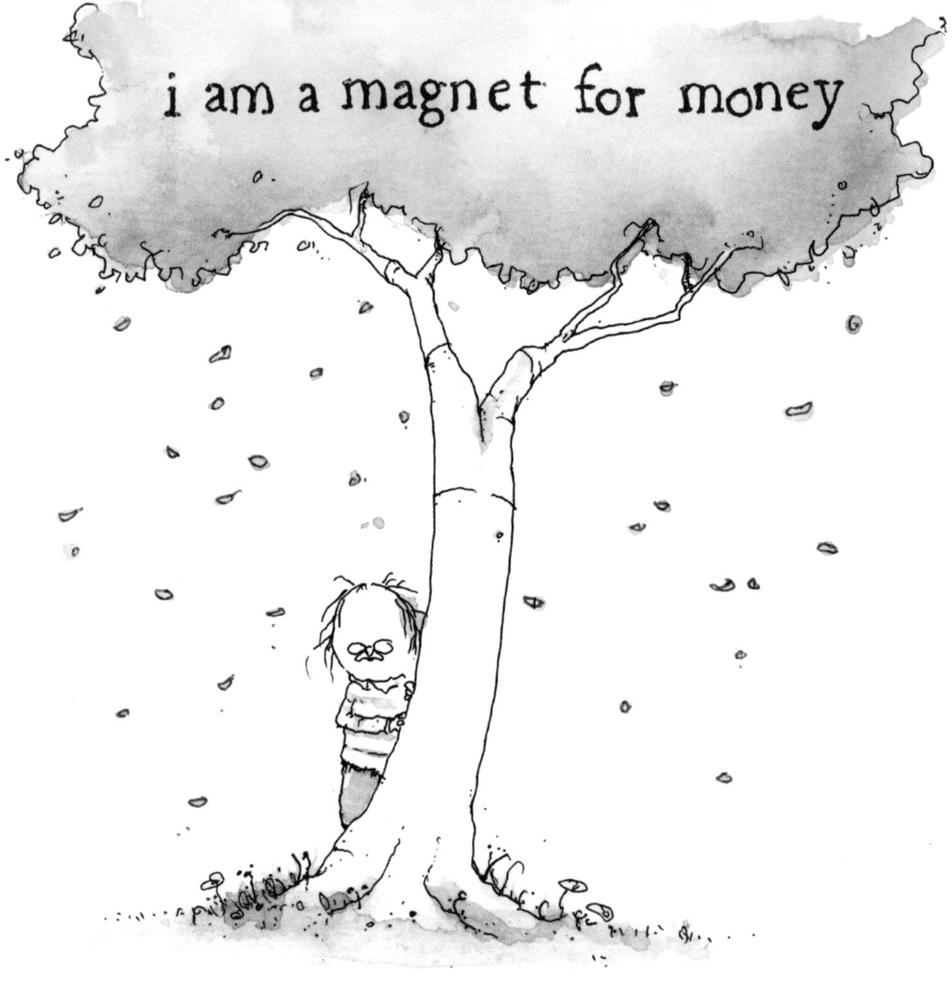
i am a magnet for money

it finds me wherever i am

i forgive myself for past mistakes

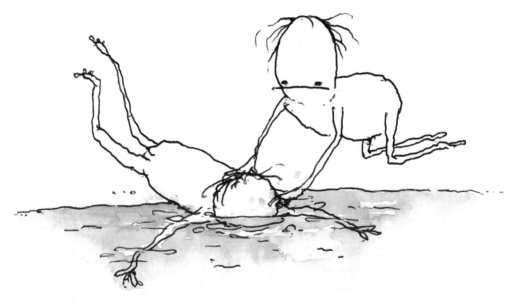

i bathe myself in a river of compassion

i surround myself with those
who see the best in me

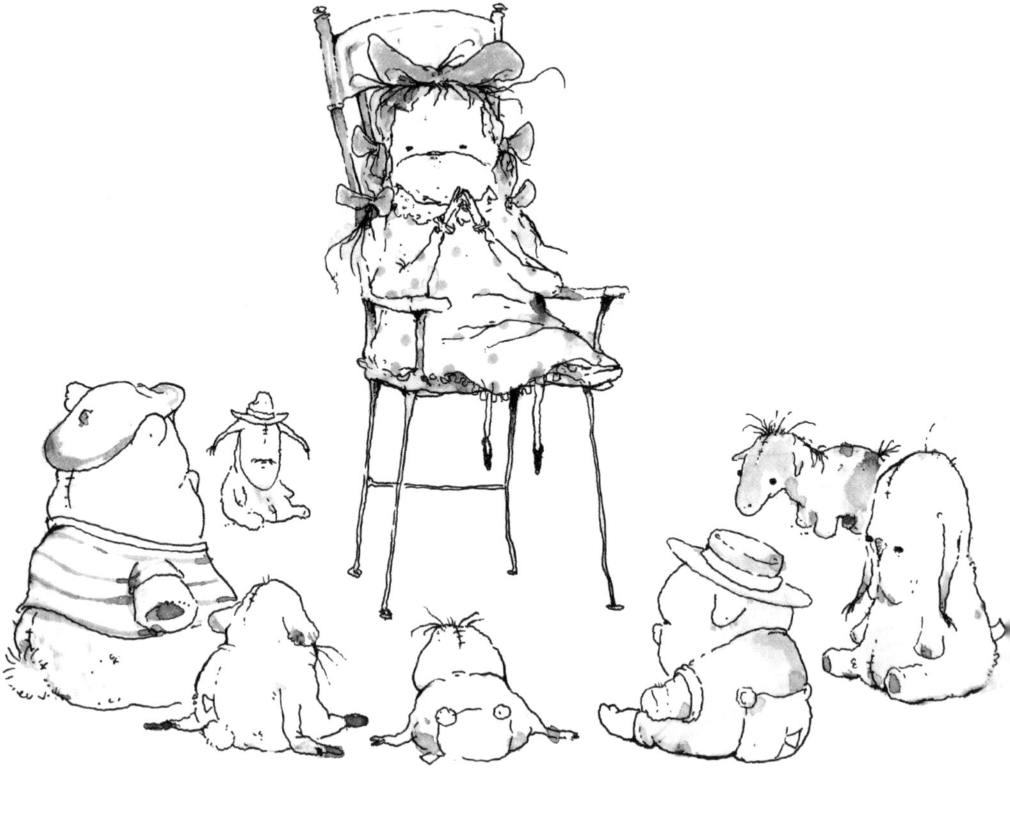

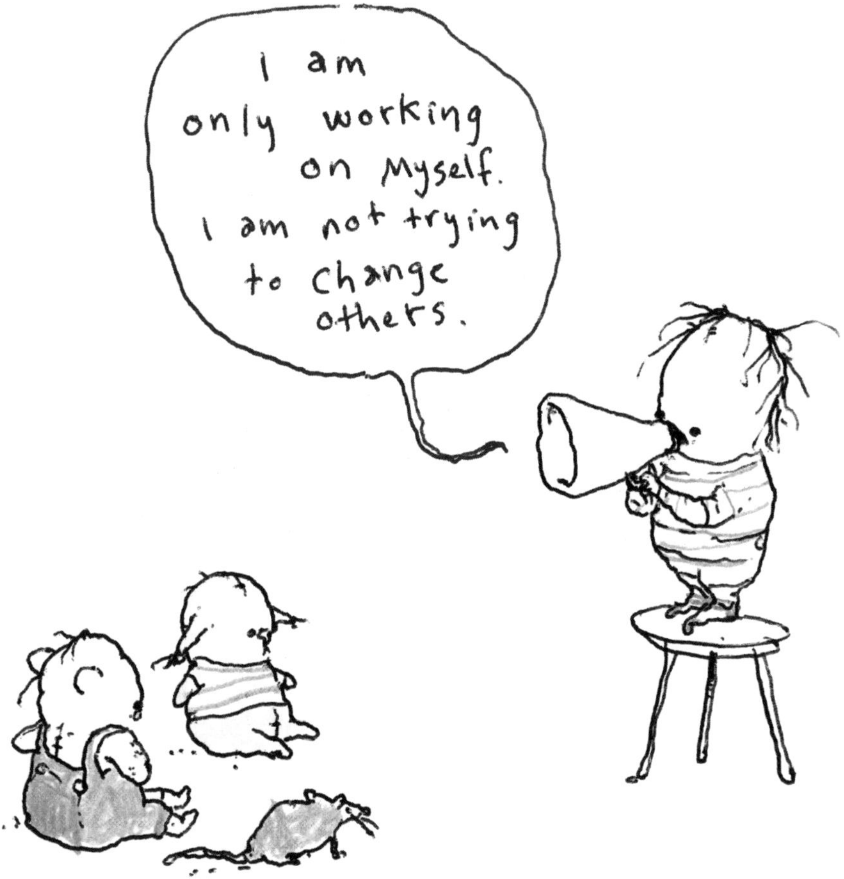
I am only working on Myself. I am not trying to change others.

i am open to sharing

i let go of my need for control

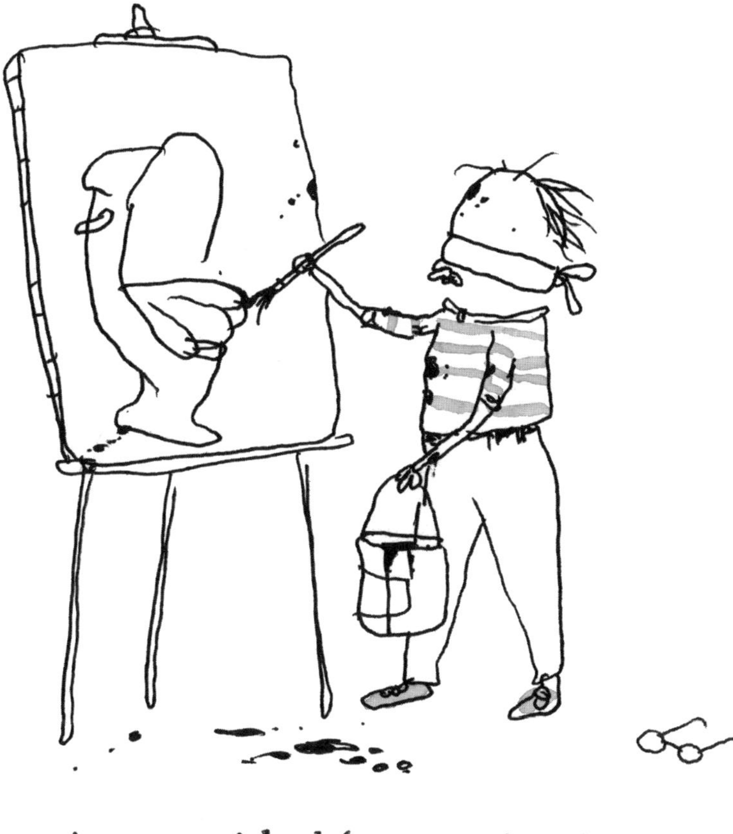

i am guided by my instincts

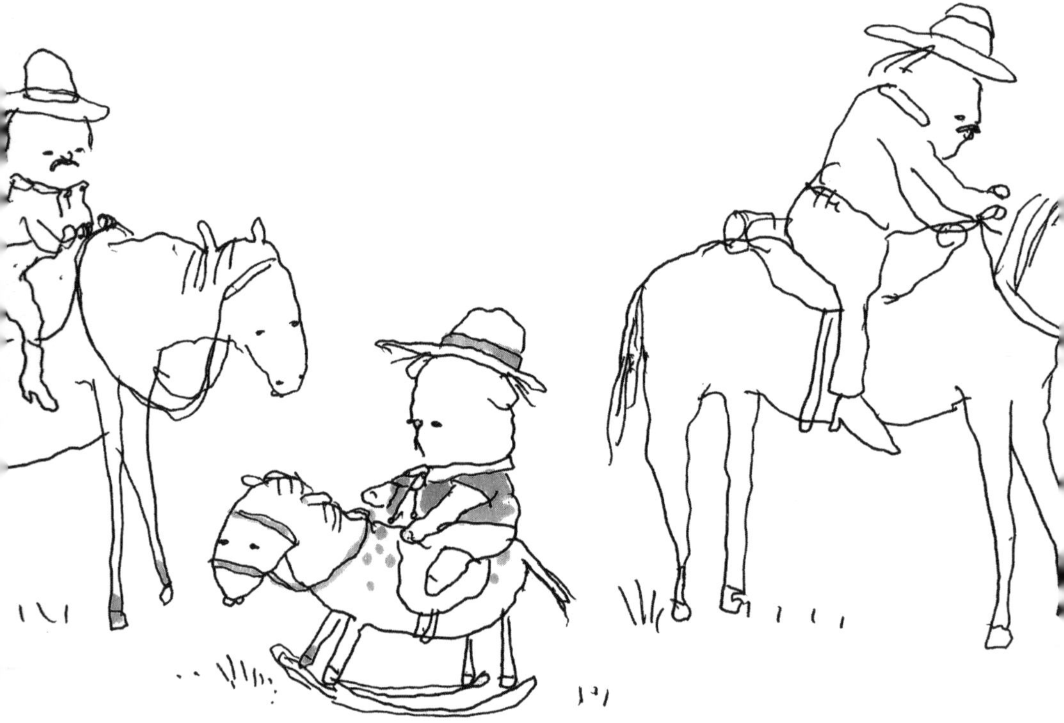

i am following my own trail

i am not
overwhelmed
by choice

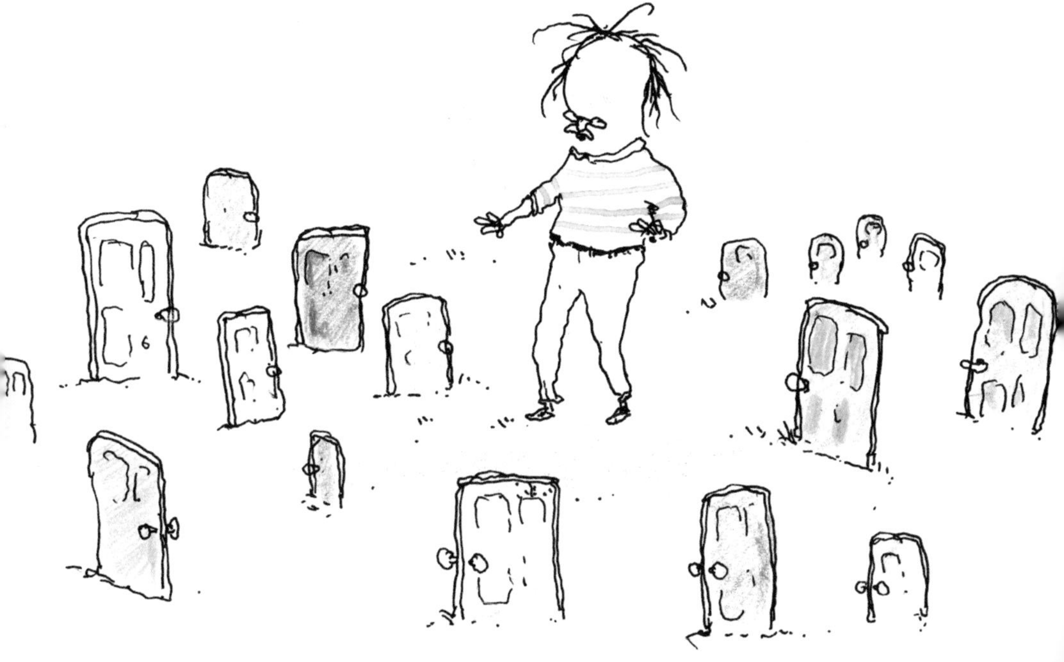

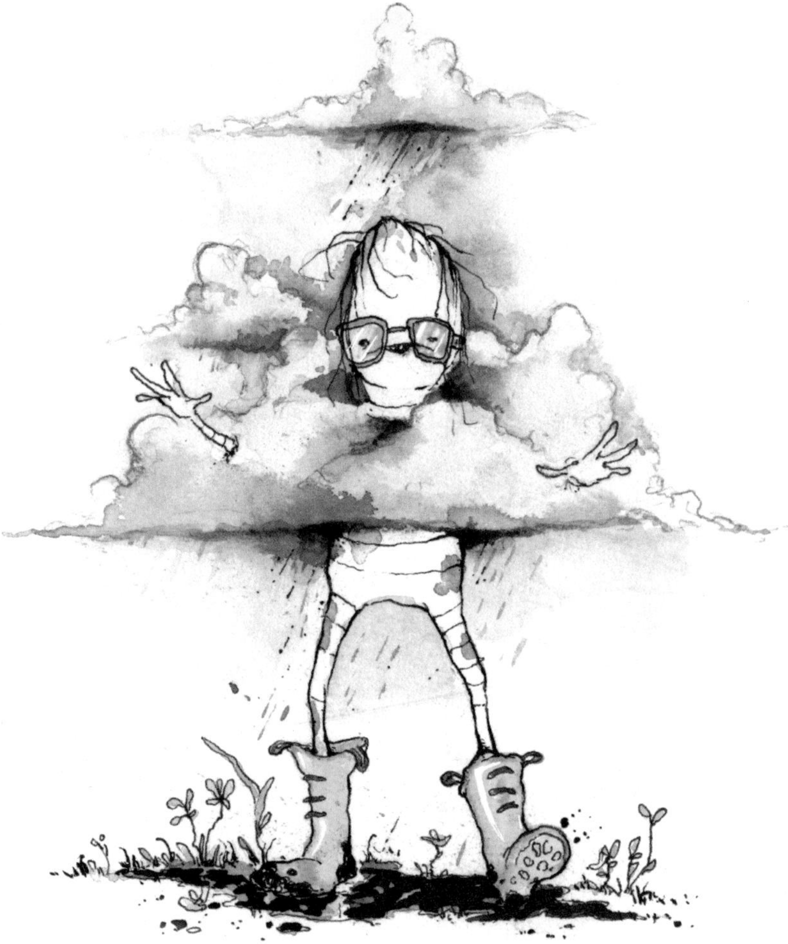

i can handle any storm

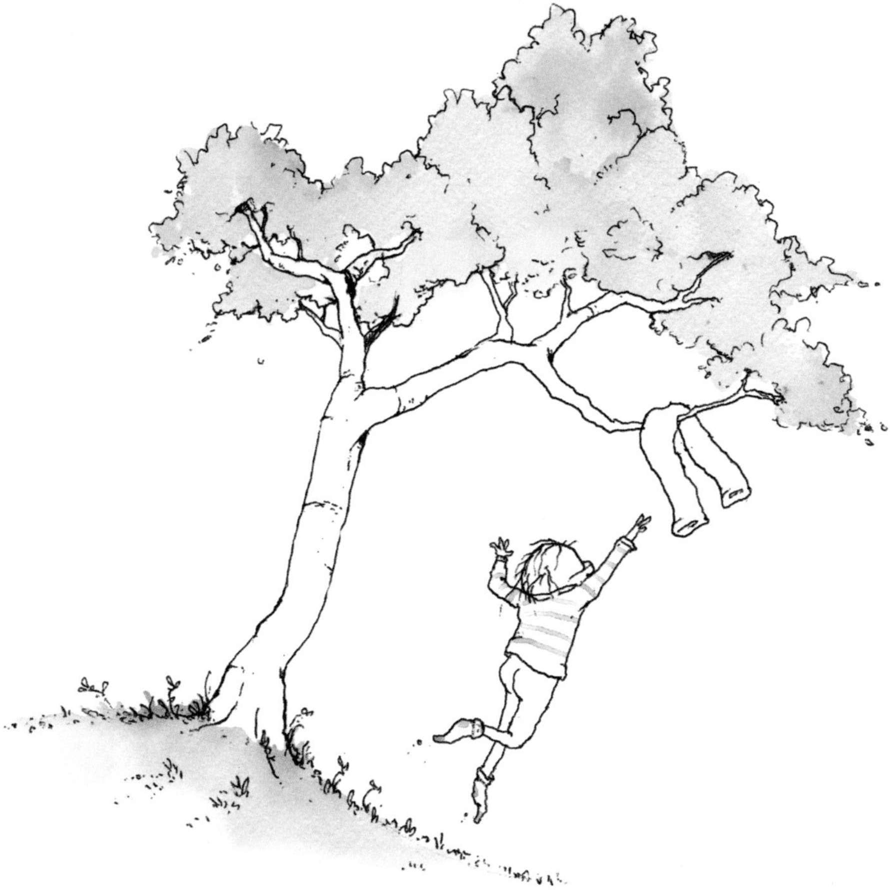

i accept the challenges life brings me

i use my
journal
every day

I want to
walk into
... the ocean

i treat myself with kindness

i am submerged in an ocean of
love and acceptance

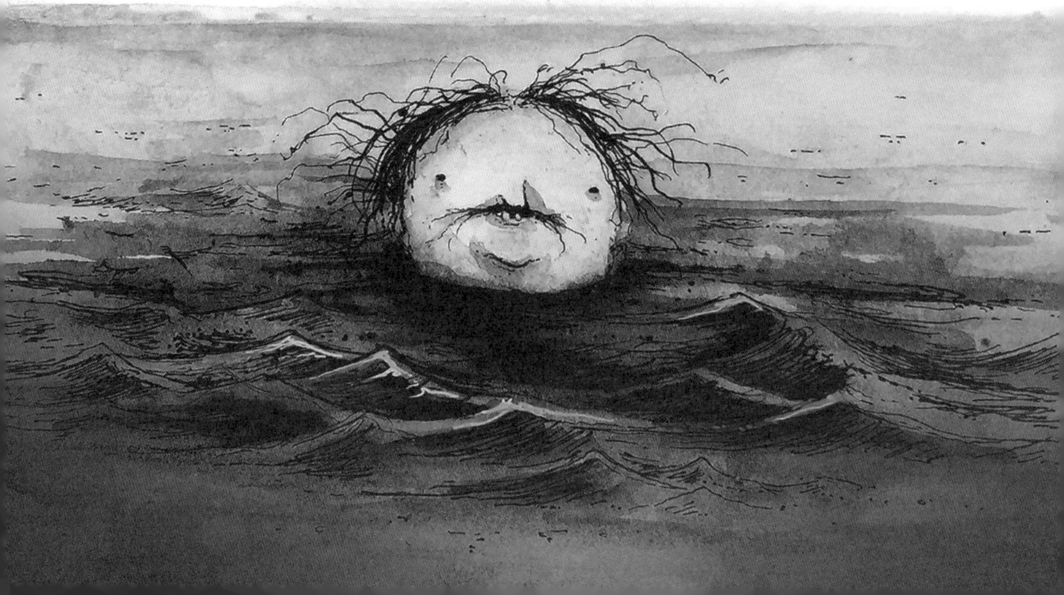

i'm where
i'm meant
to be

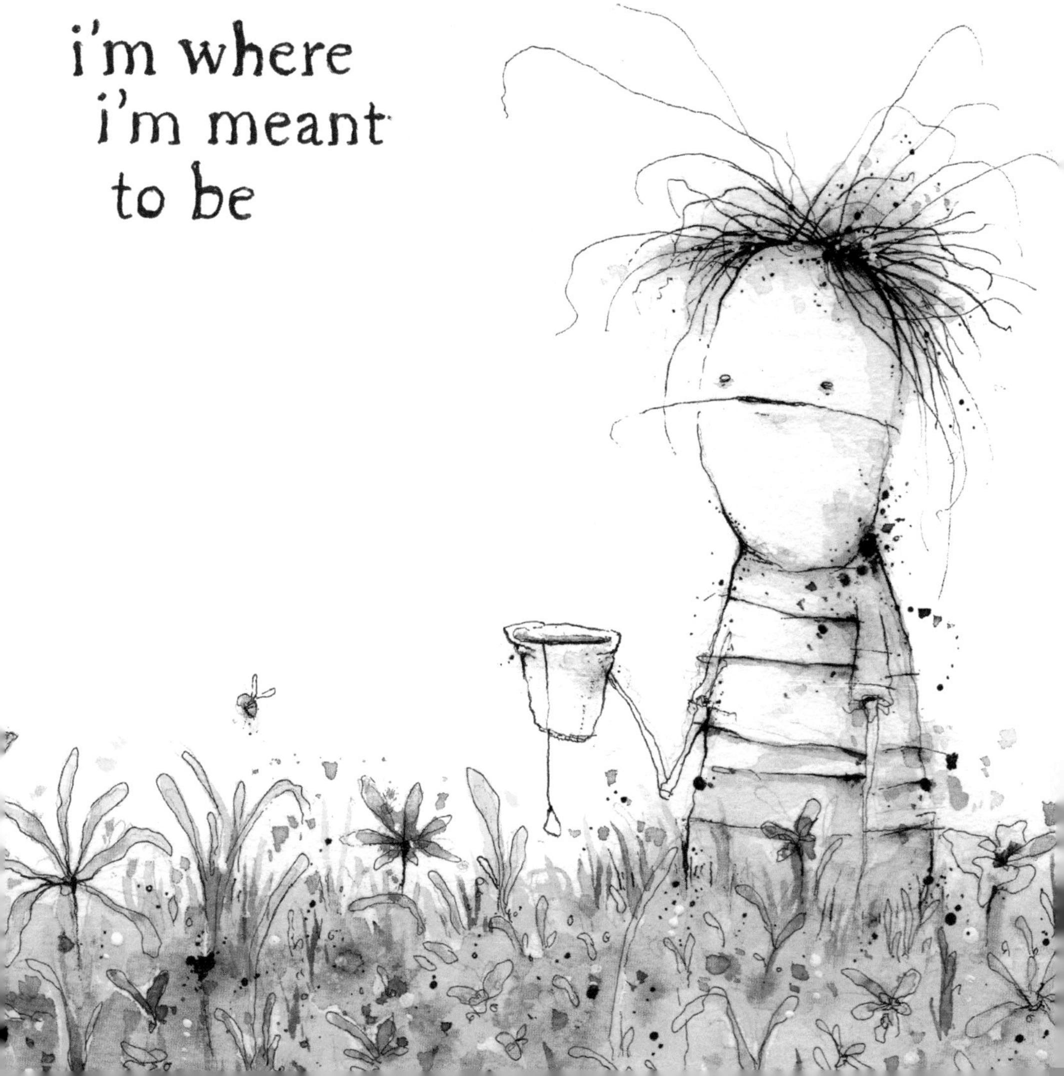

my gratitude list
grows longer every day

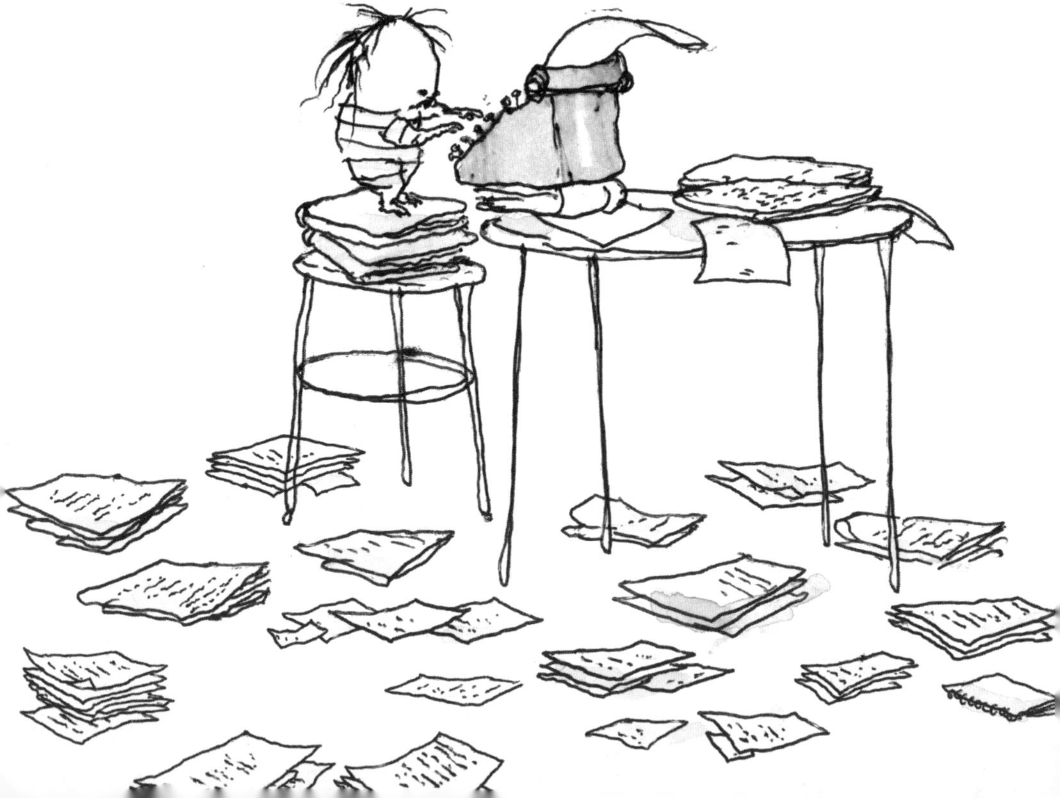

i make peace
with my past self

i can
overcome
any obstacle

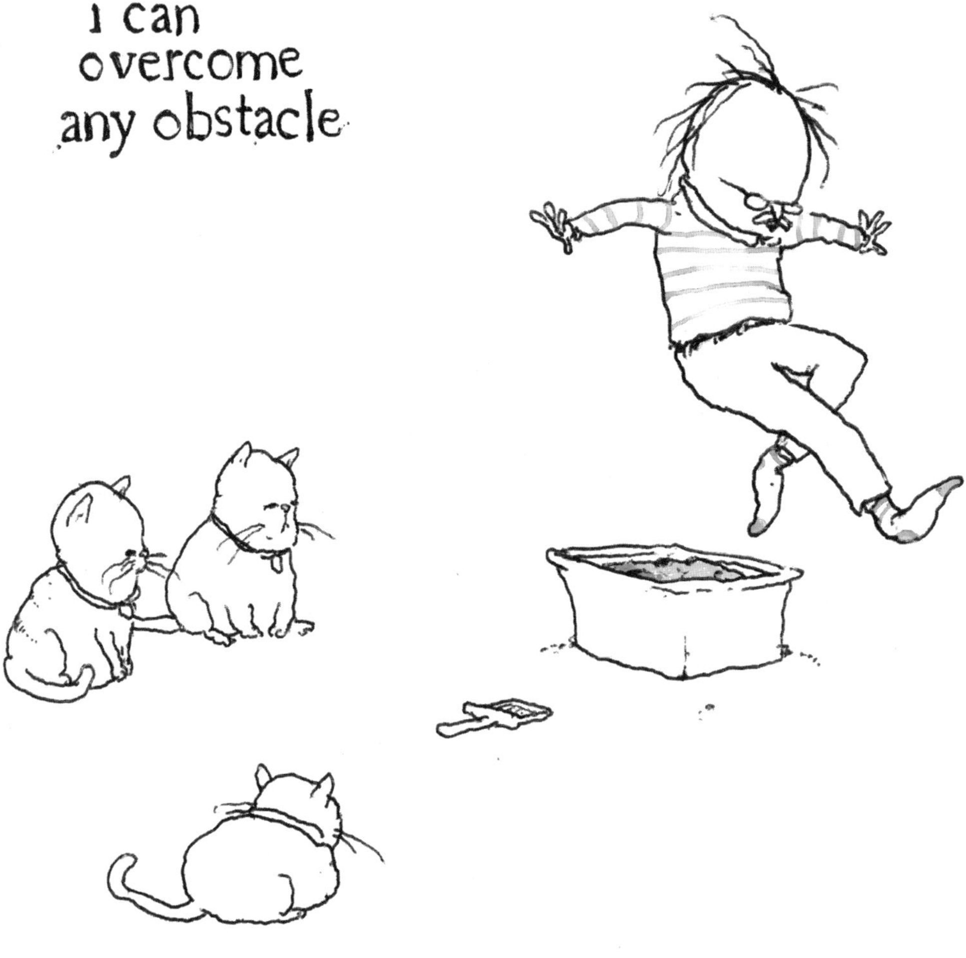

challenges
bring out
the best in me

i accept
failure
with grace

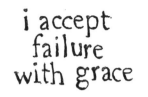

i make
new friends
easily

others are drawn to my
charisma and good nature

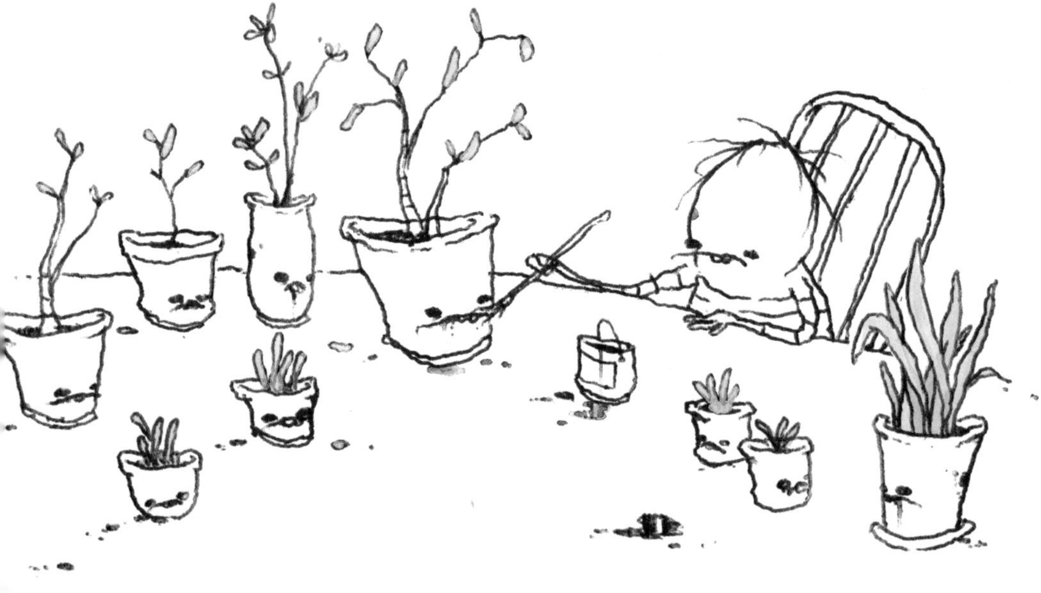

i create
myself

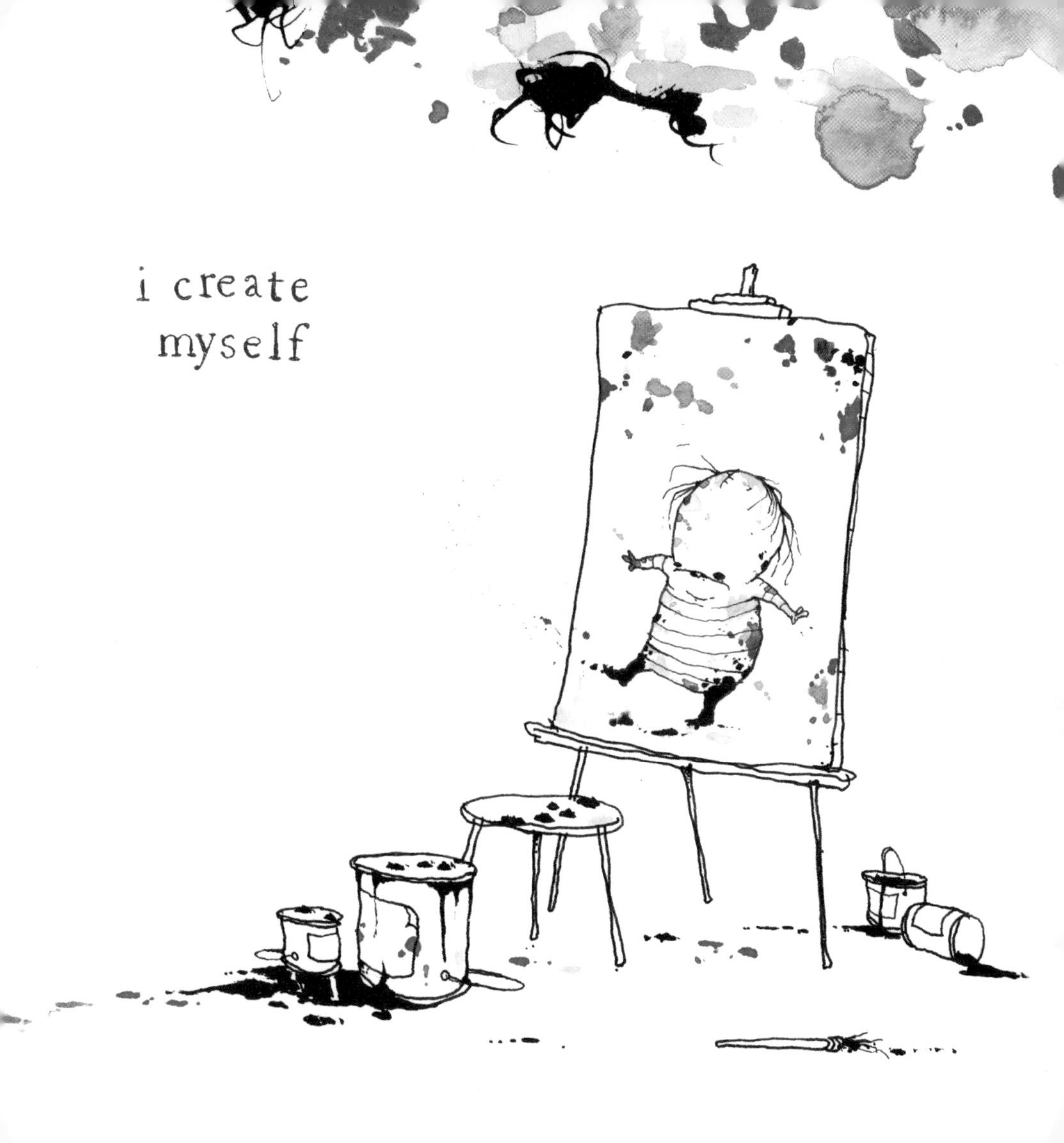

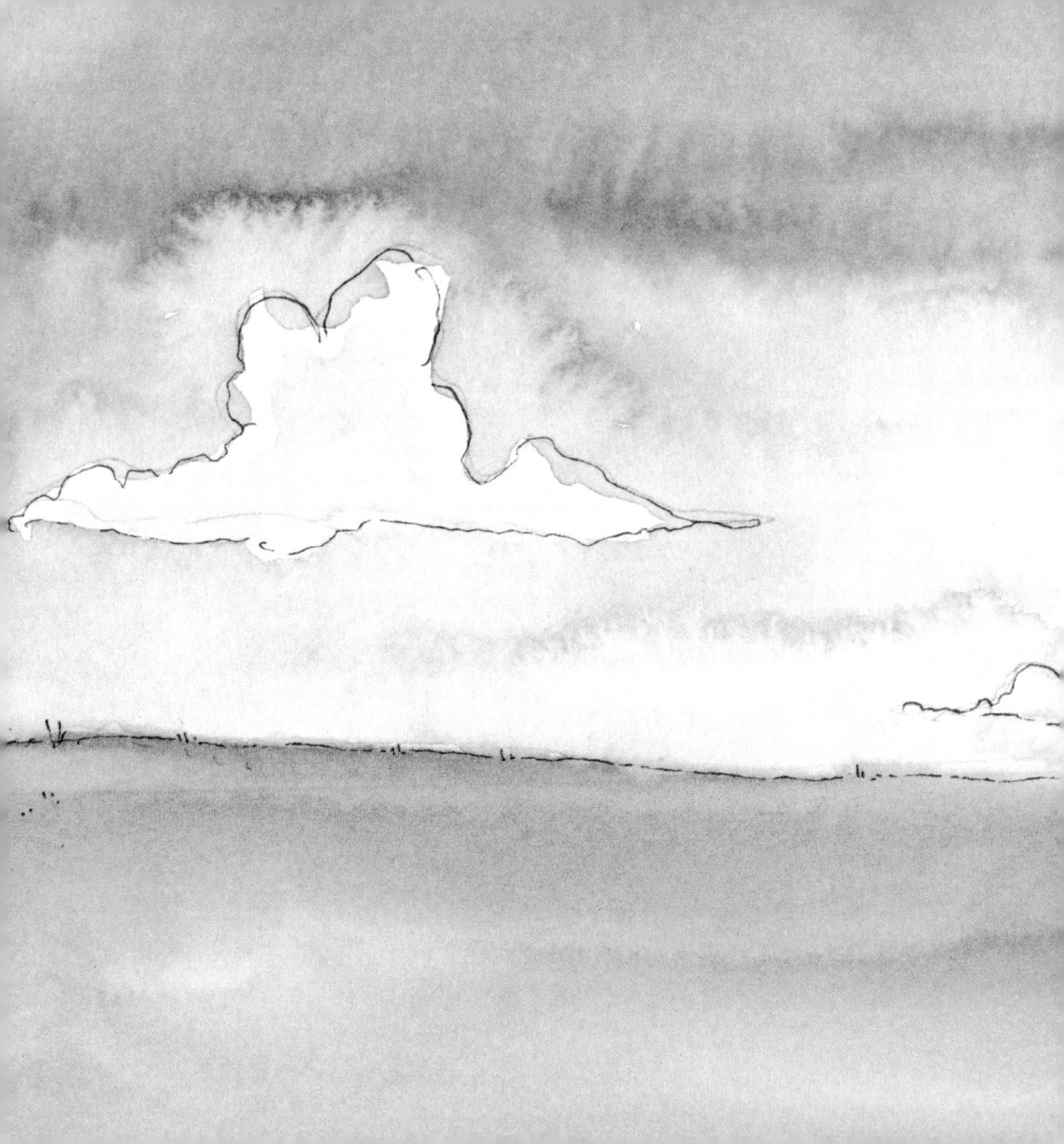

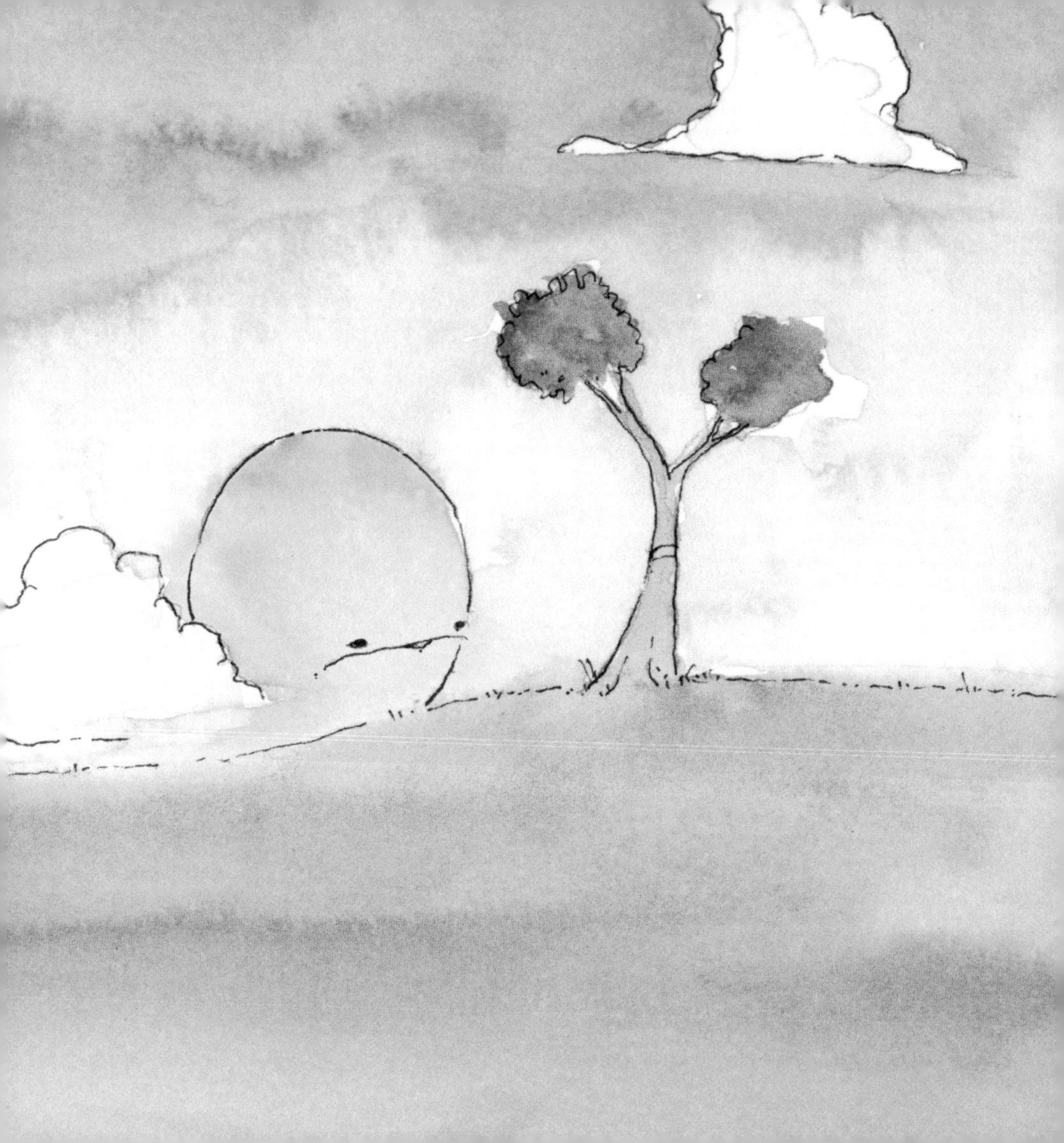

i fill my mind
with new ideas

i am always
learning

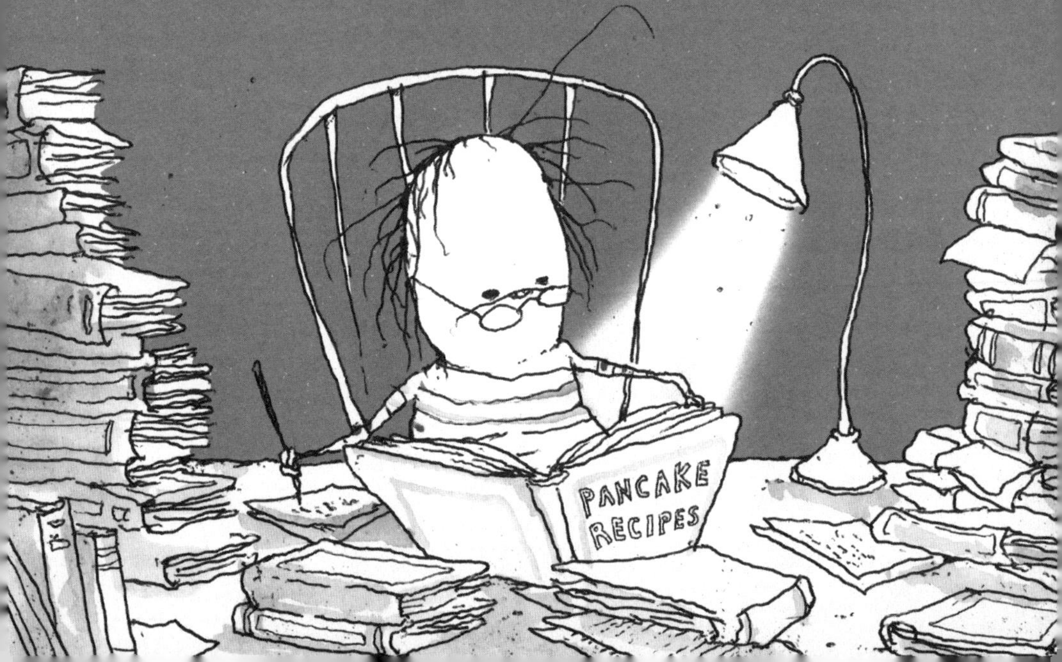
PANCAKE
RECIPES

i allow myself
to make bad art

i make room
in myself for
imperfection

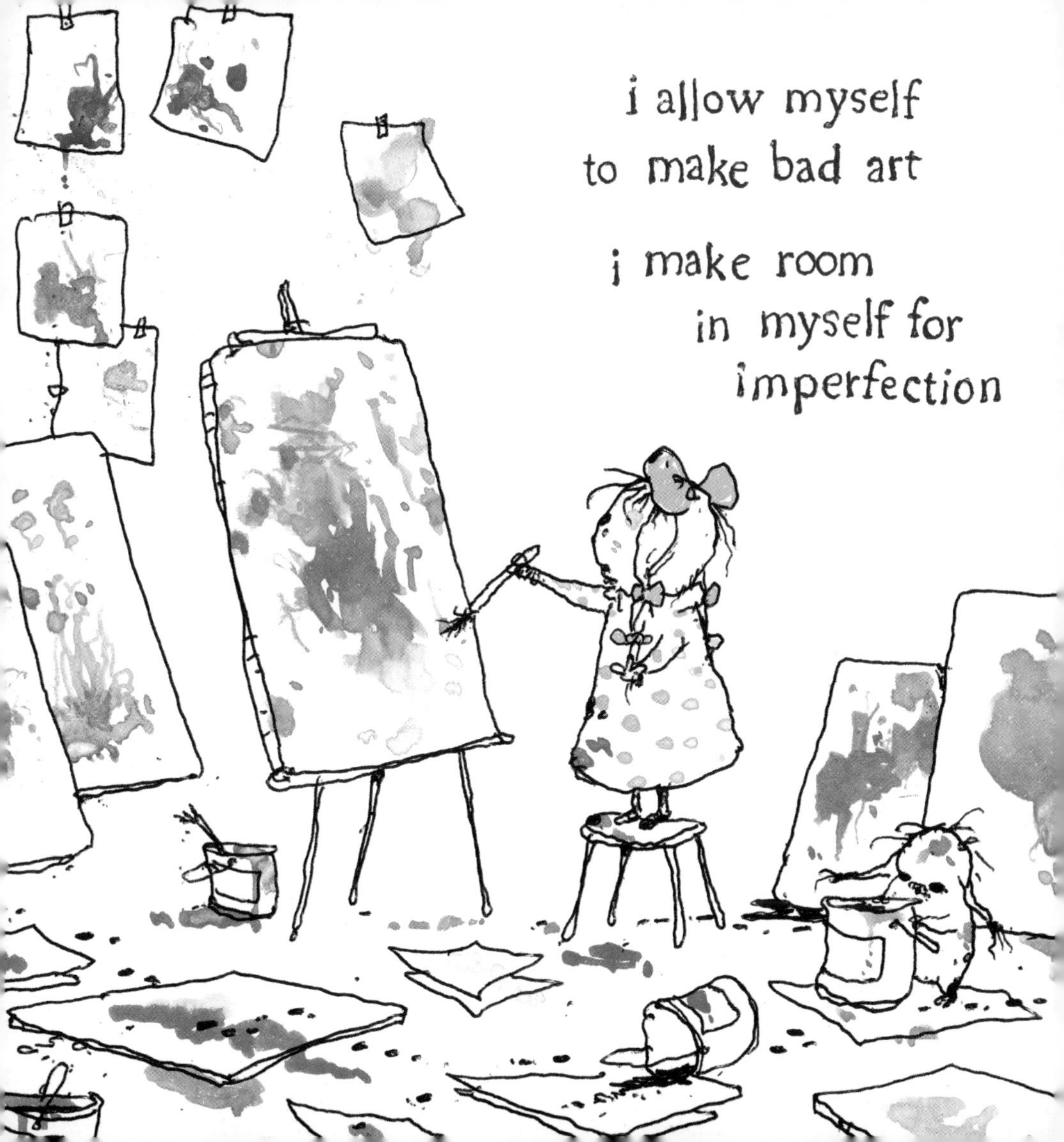

my
humility
is growing
every
day

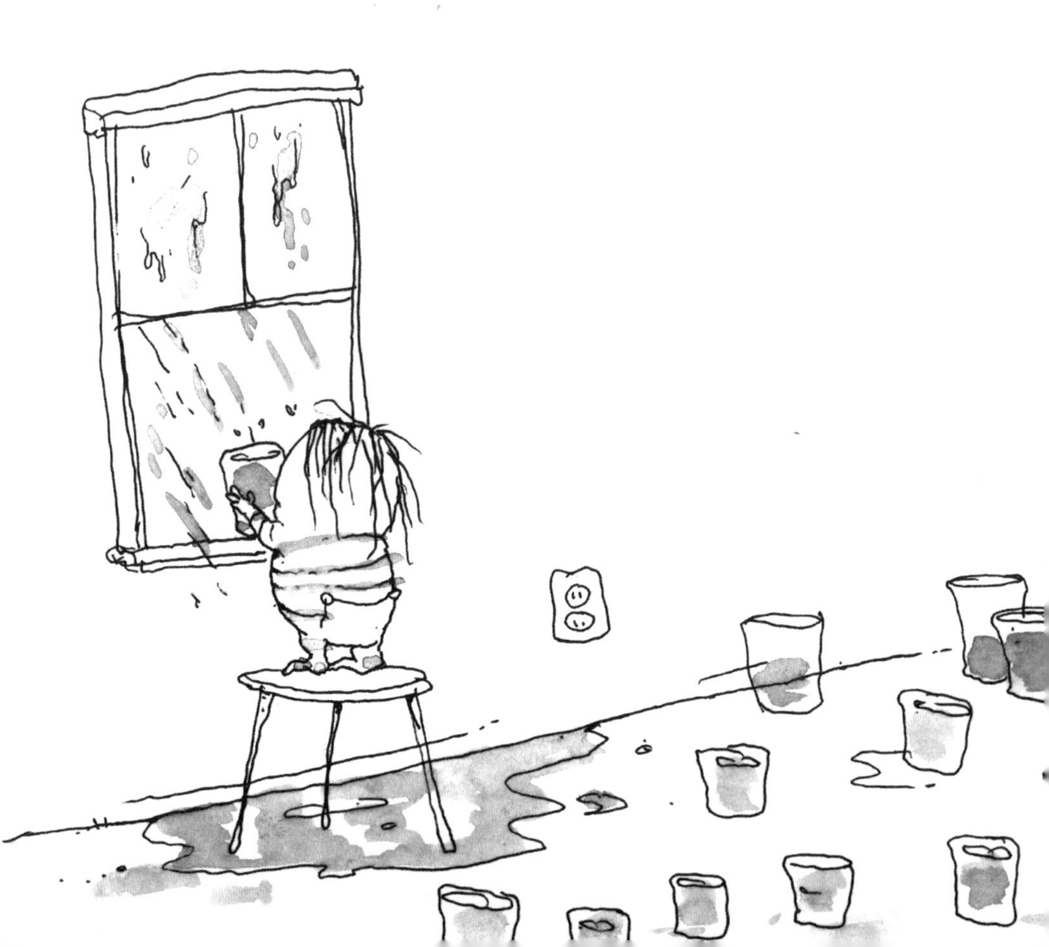

i take advantage
of new opportunities

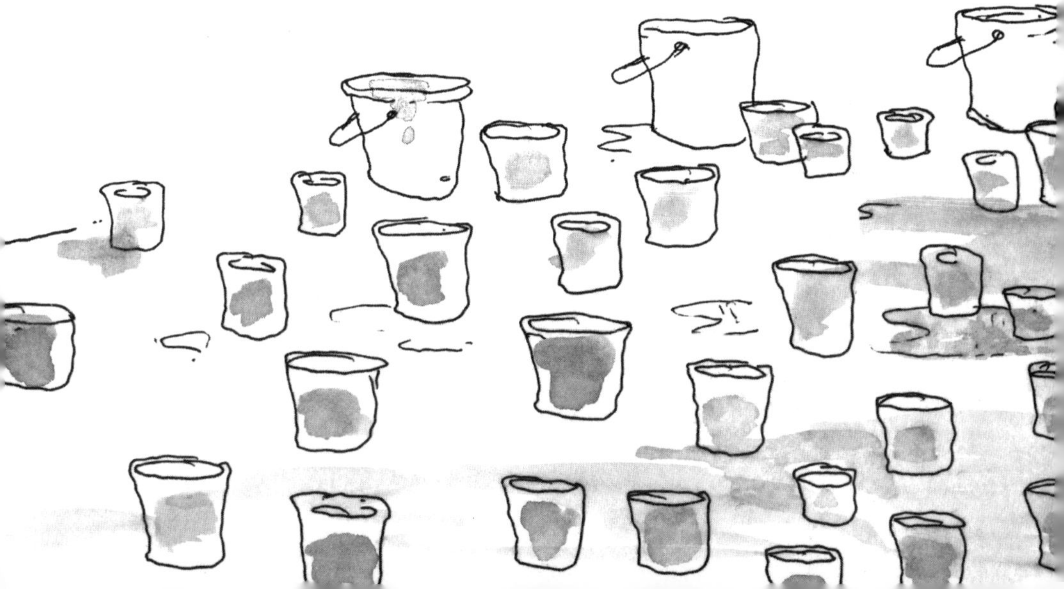

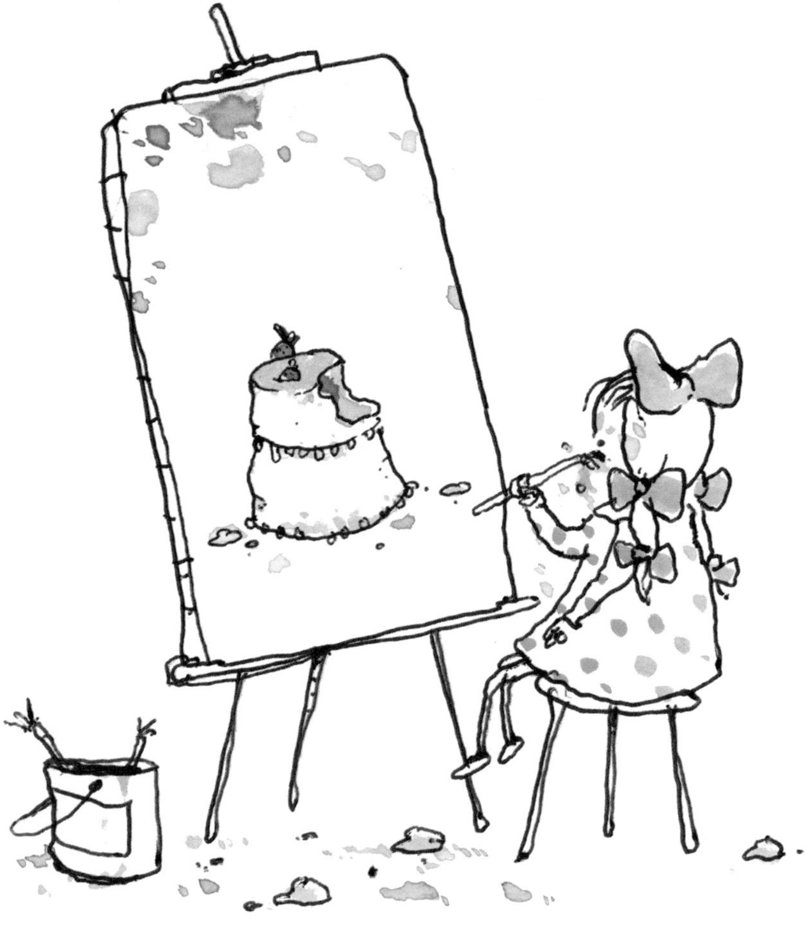

i use my creativity for good

i am
learning
to accept
change

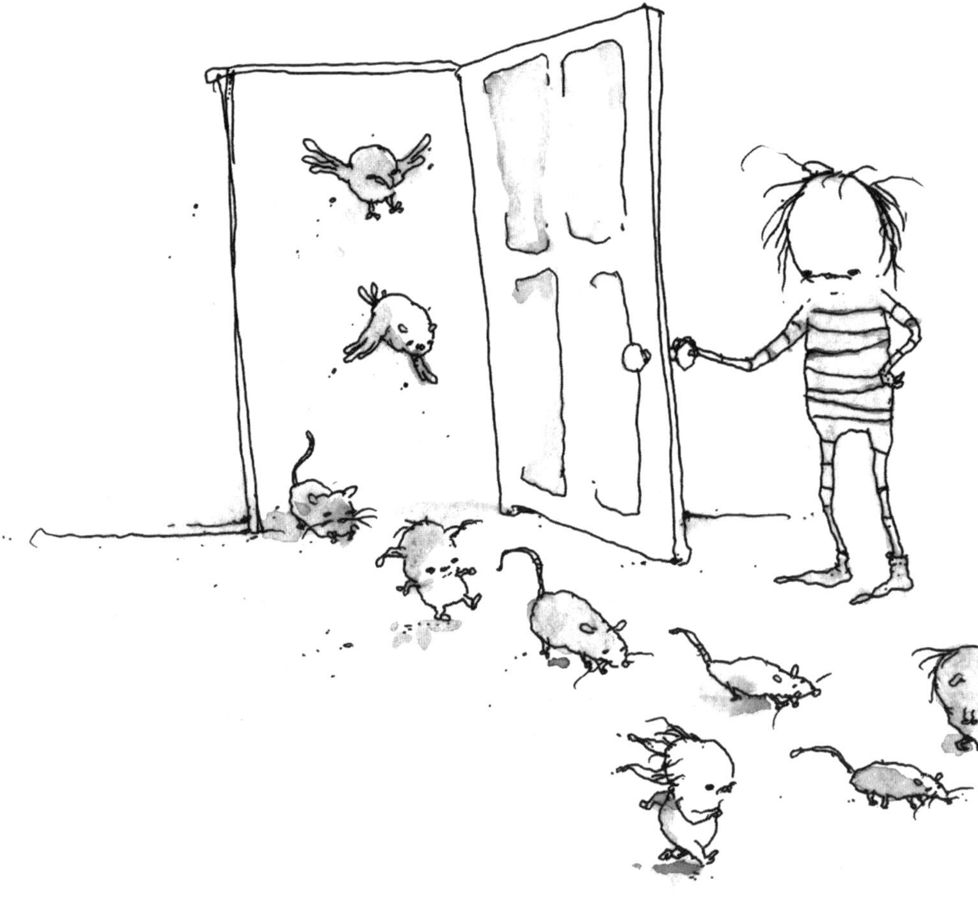

i let new
experiences
into my life

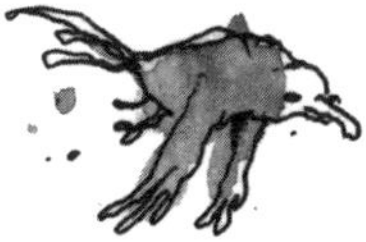

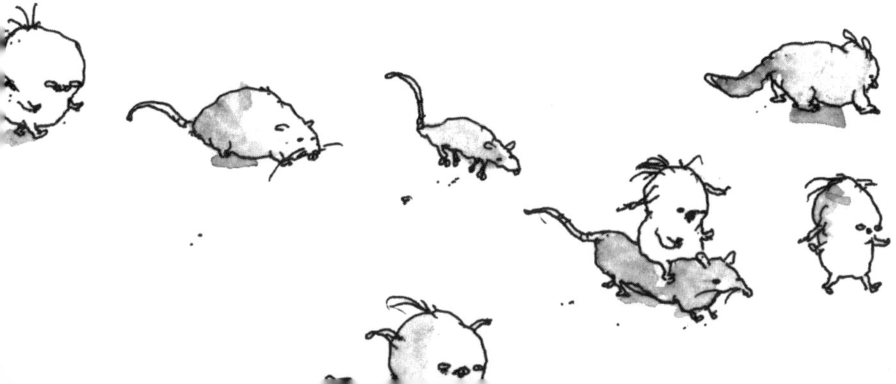

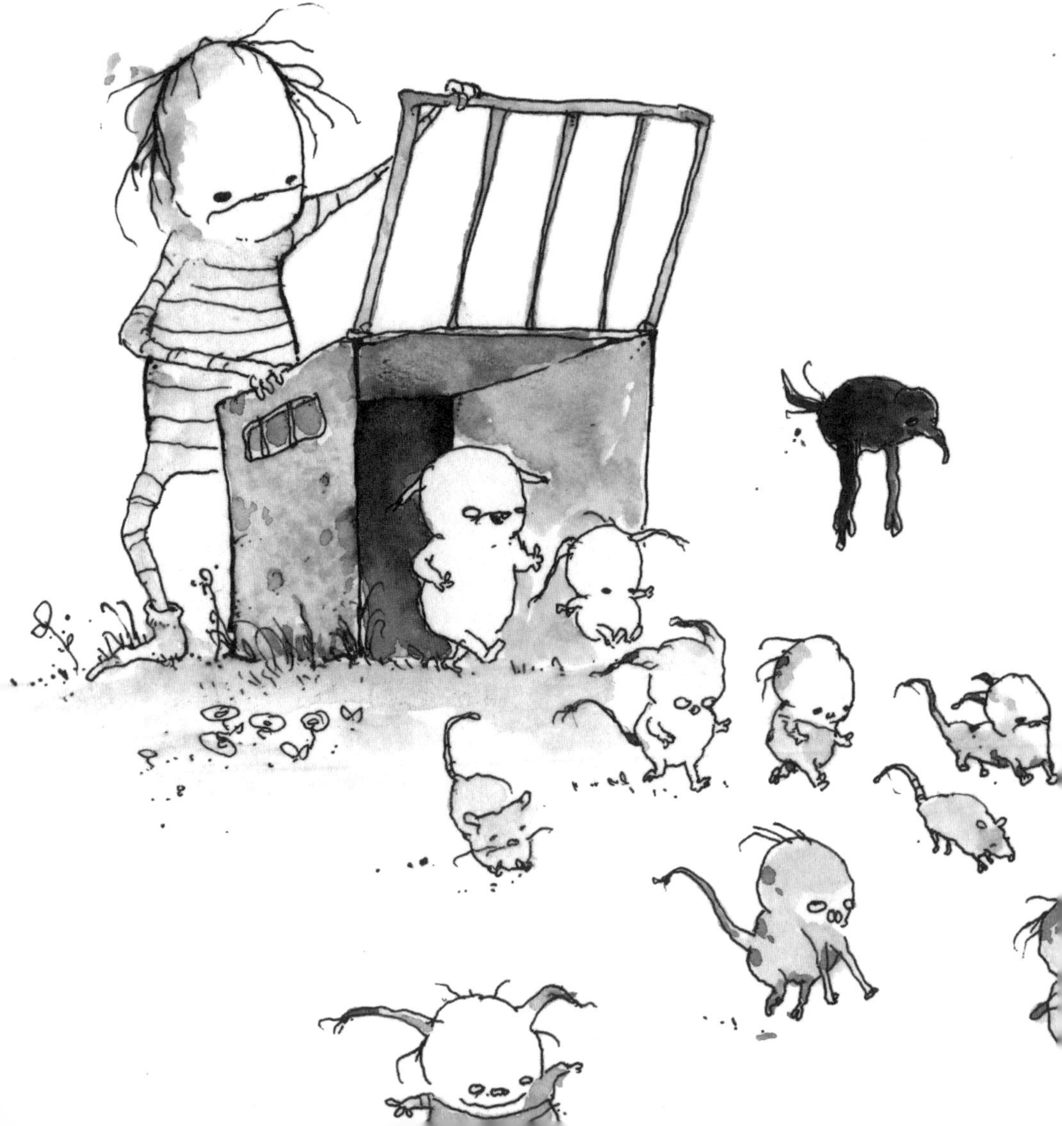

i forgive
those who have
wronged me

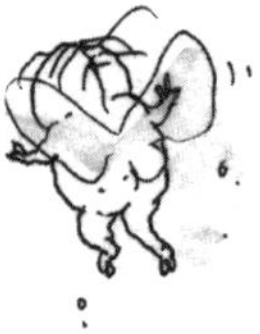

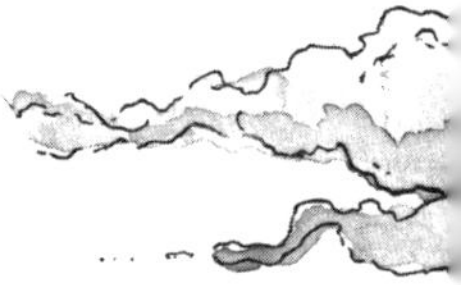

i manifest
my thoughts

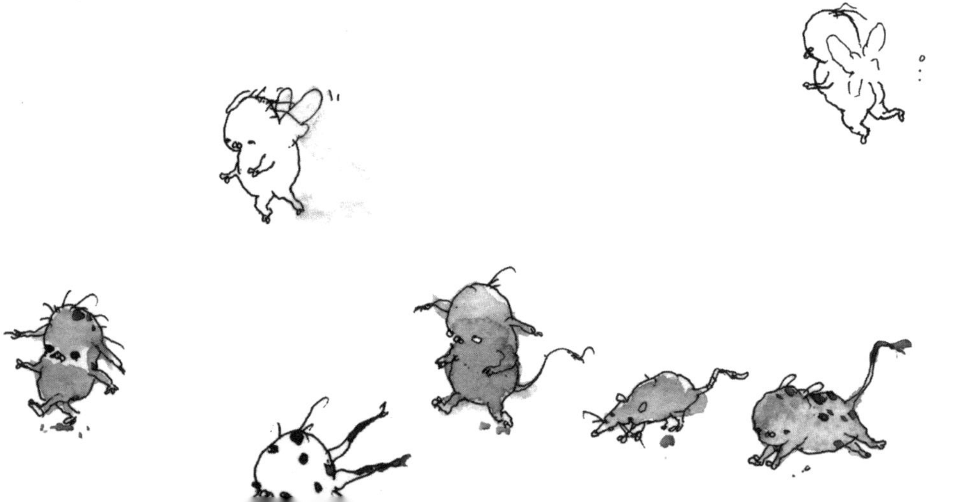

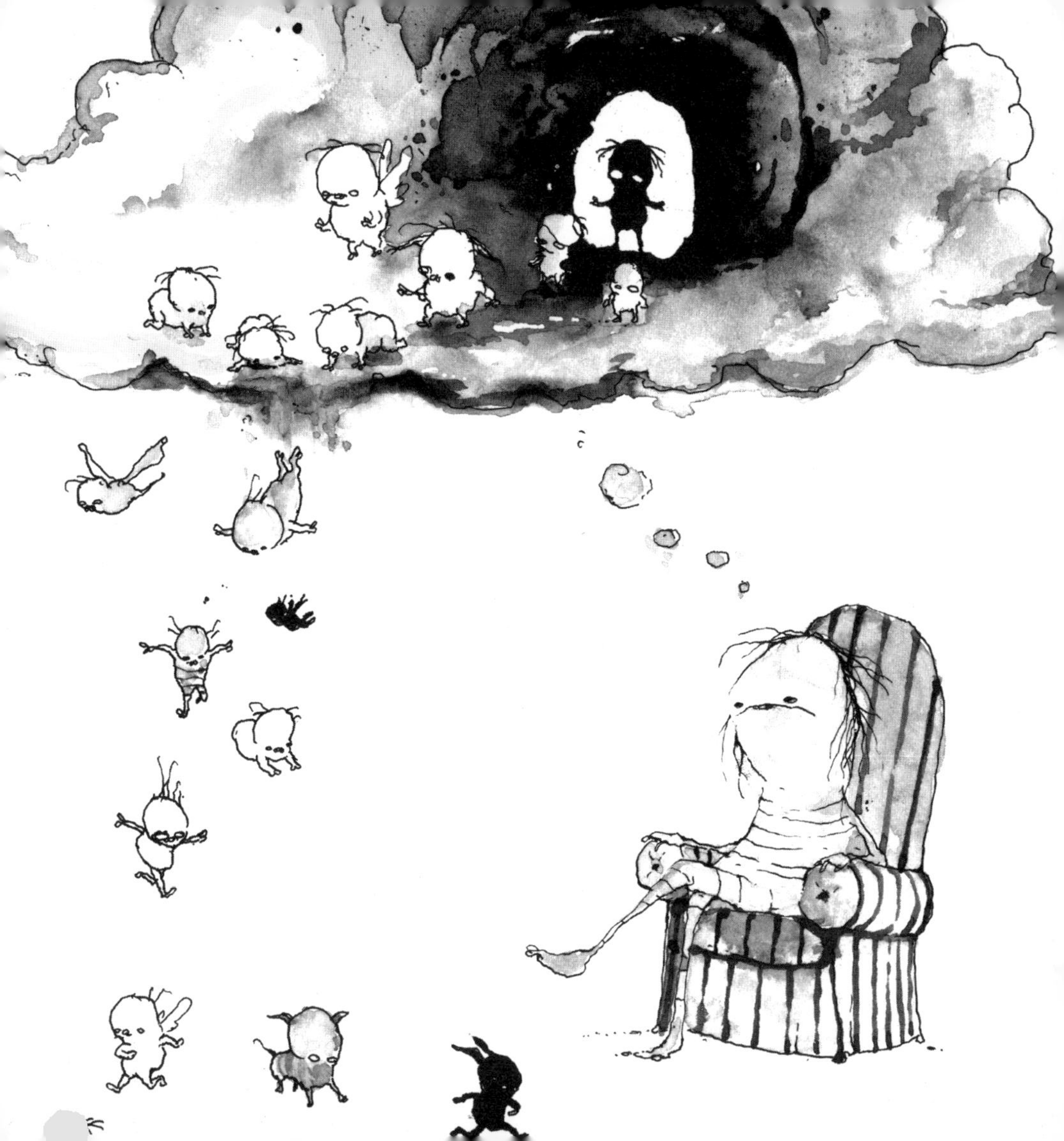

i am
open to
gifts from the
universe

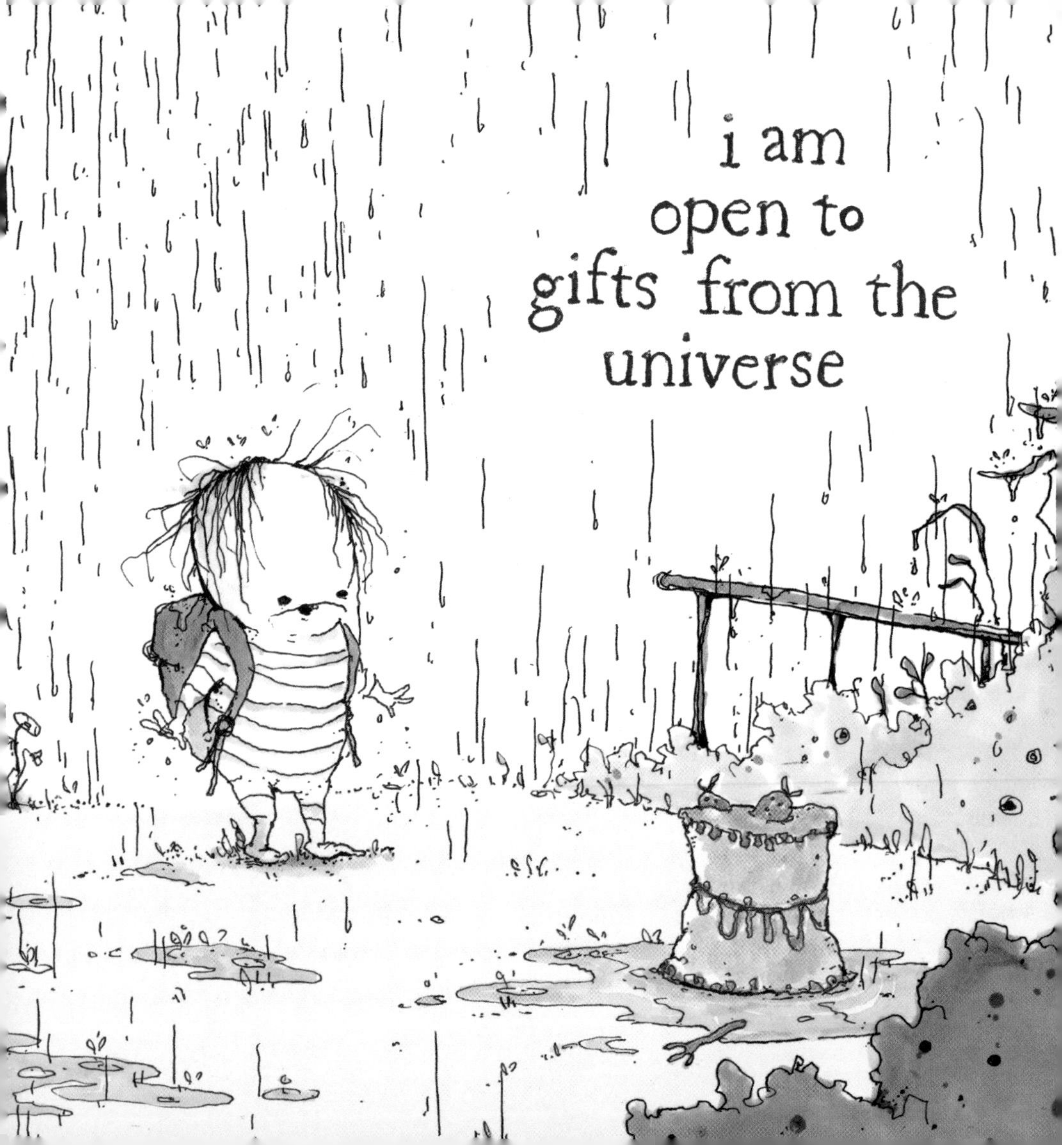

i am comfortable being alone

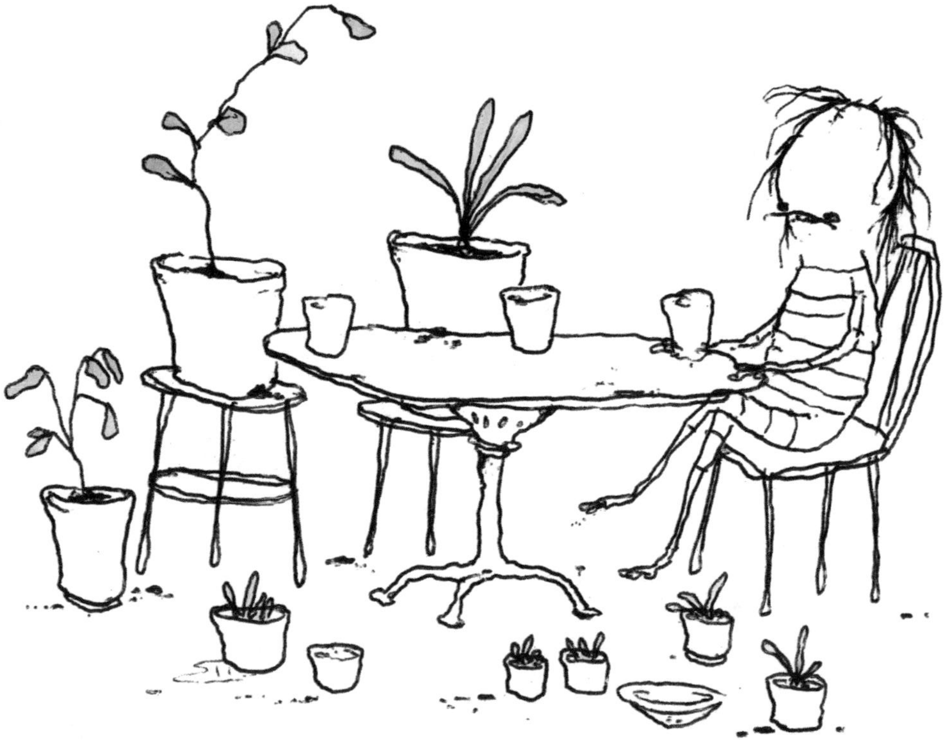

i use
visualization
to better myself

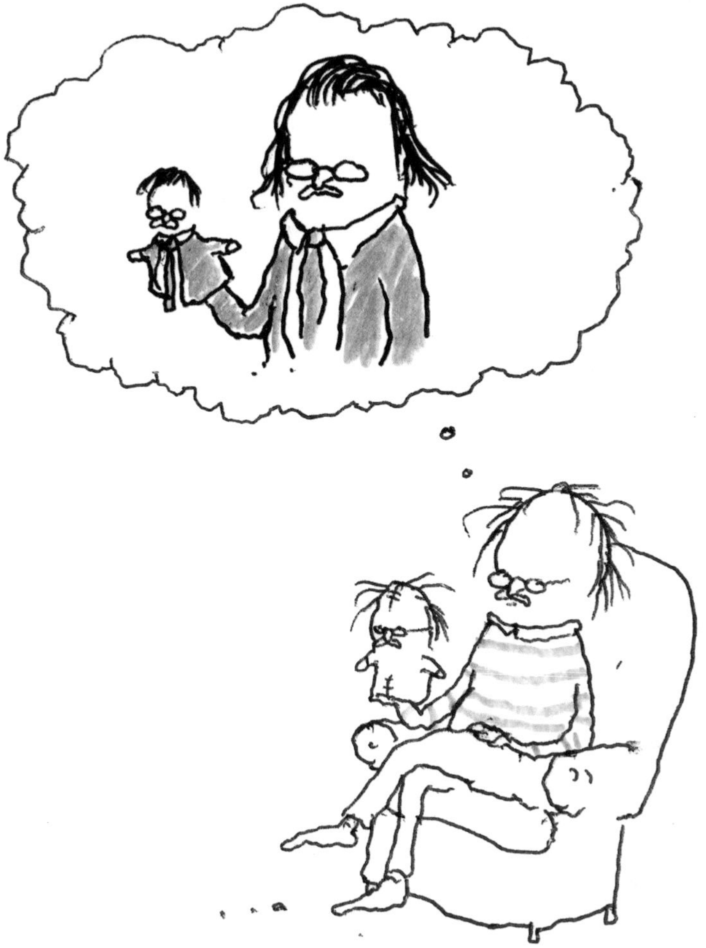

i let go of my
resentment and negativity

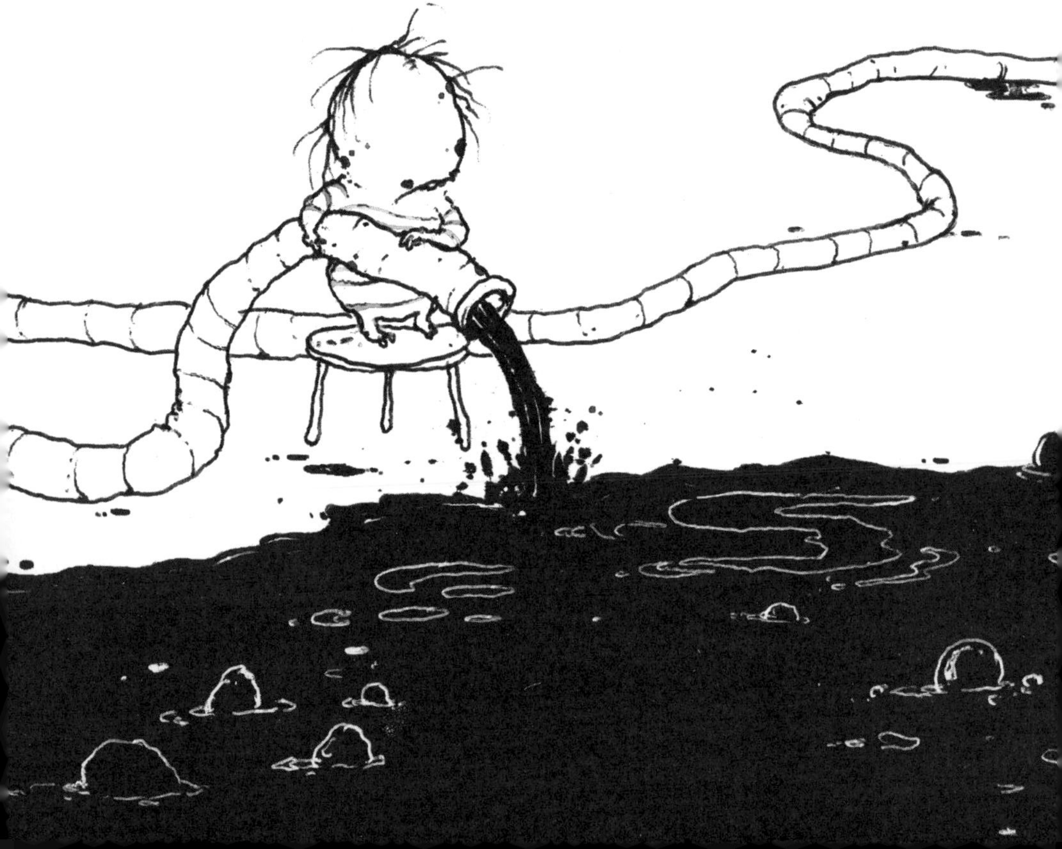

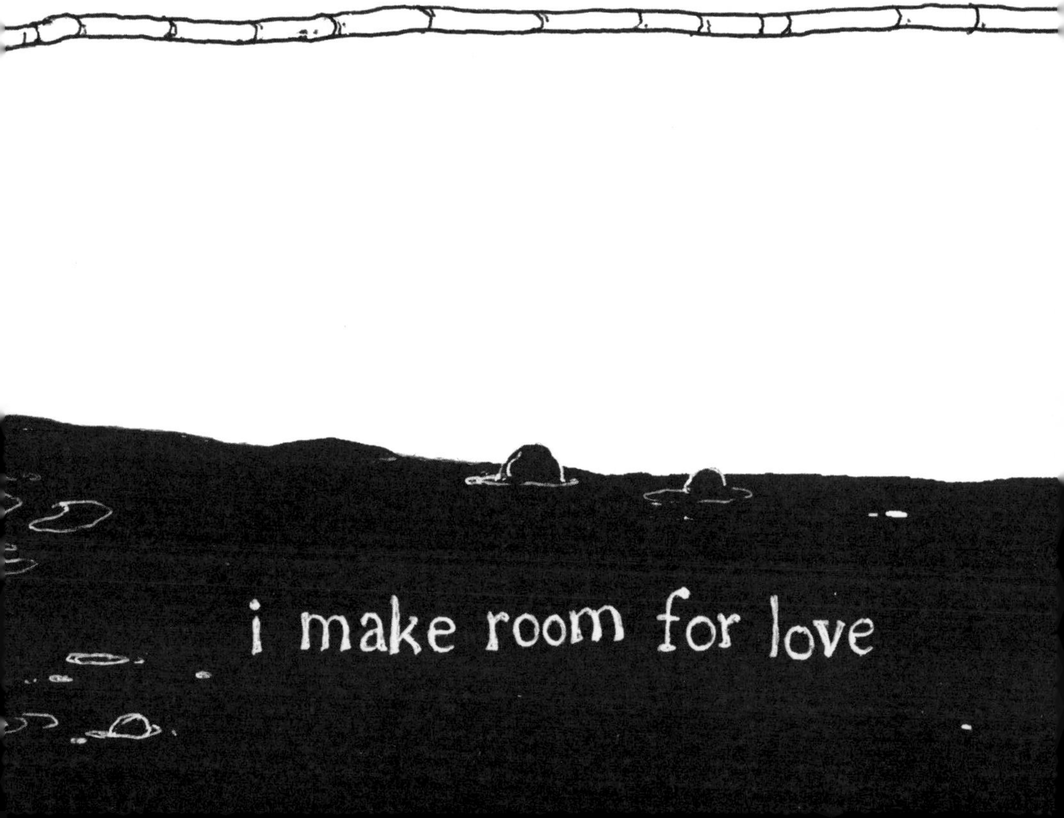
i make room for love

i face
my fears

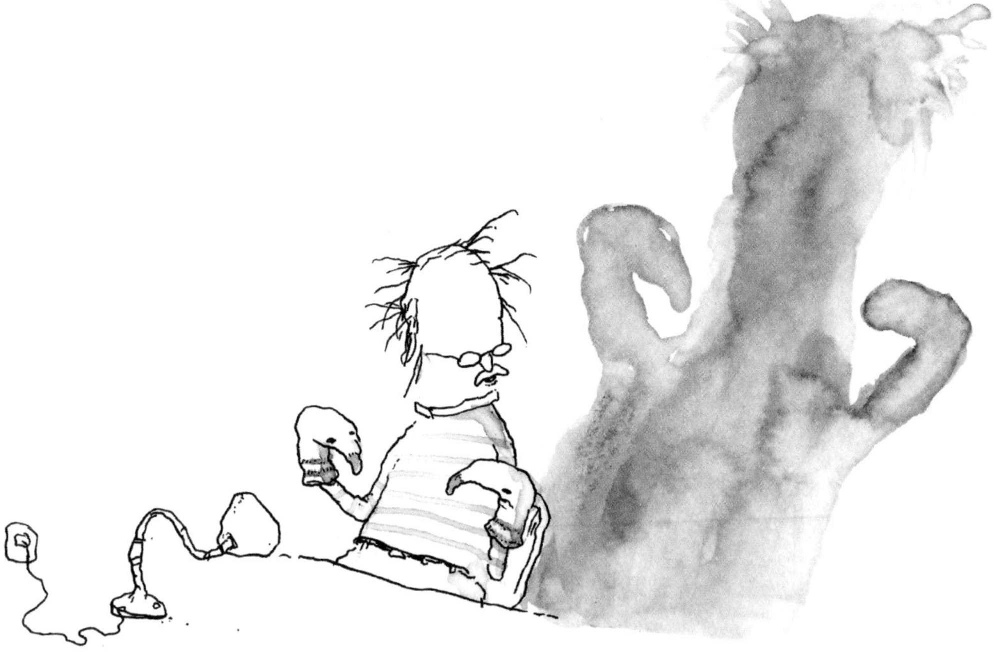

i take care
of myself

i heat up my
socks when
my feet are cold

my imagination is limitless

i draw horses without reference

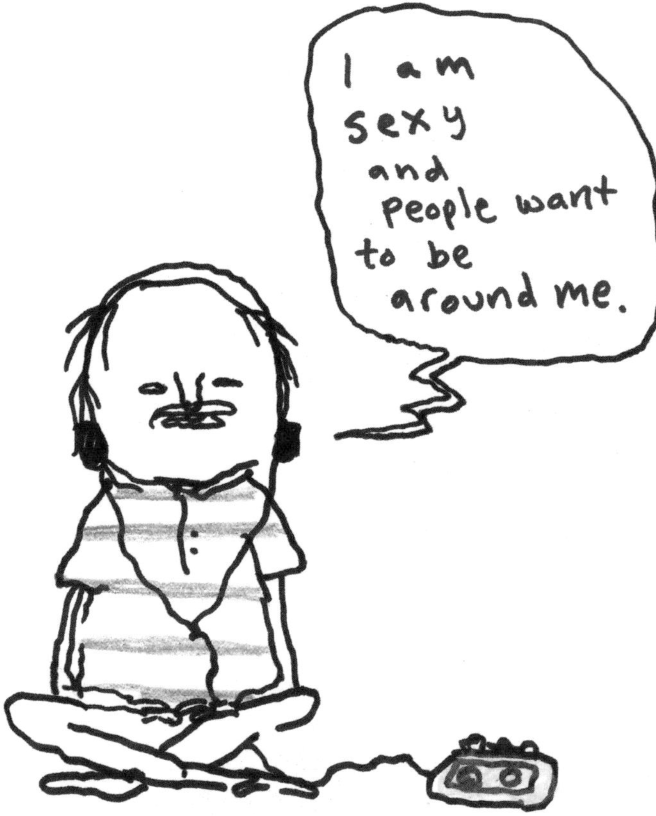
I am sexy and people want to be around me.

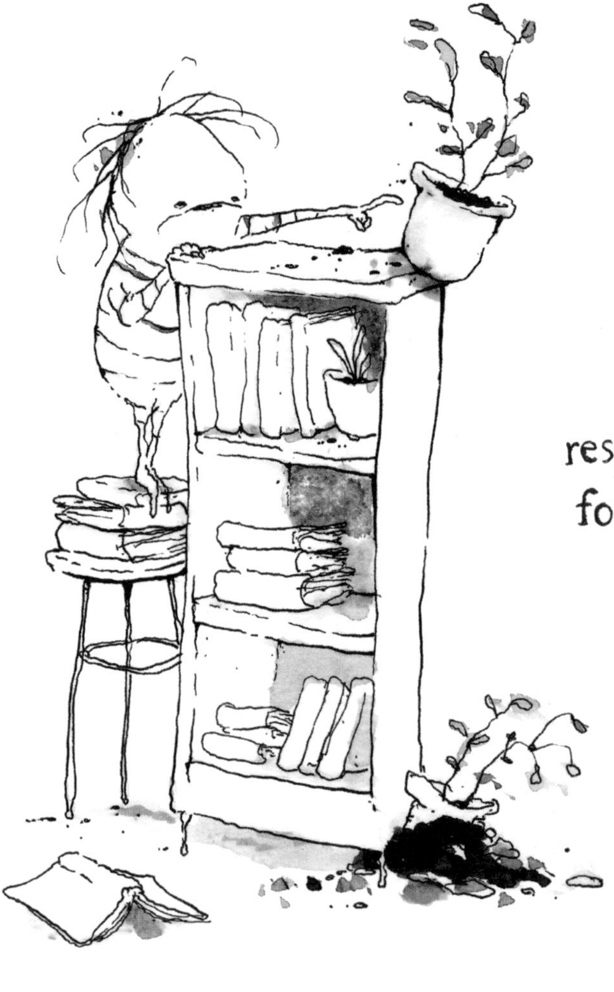

i take
responsibility
for what i've
done

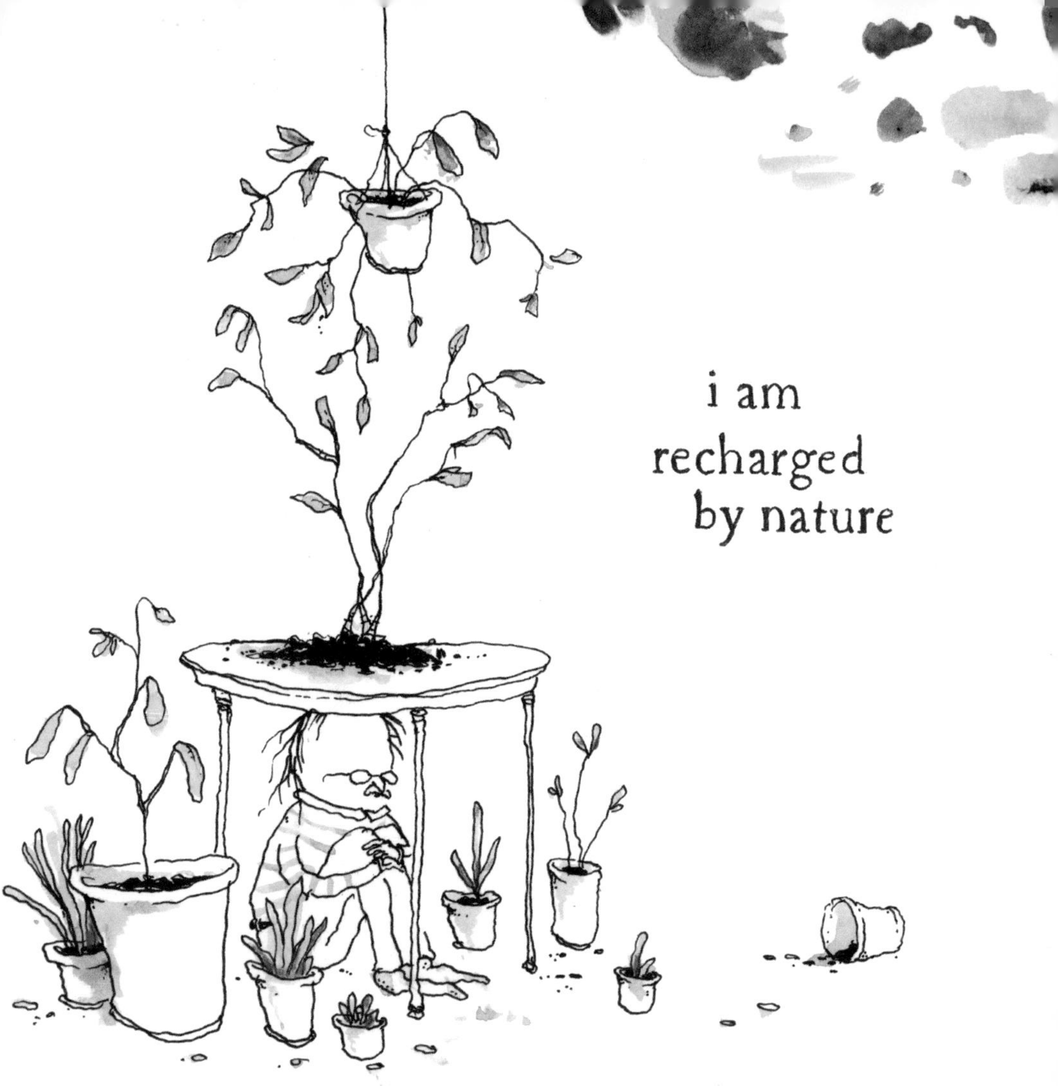

i am
recharged
by nature

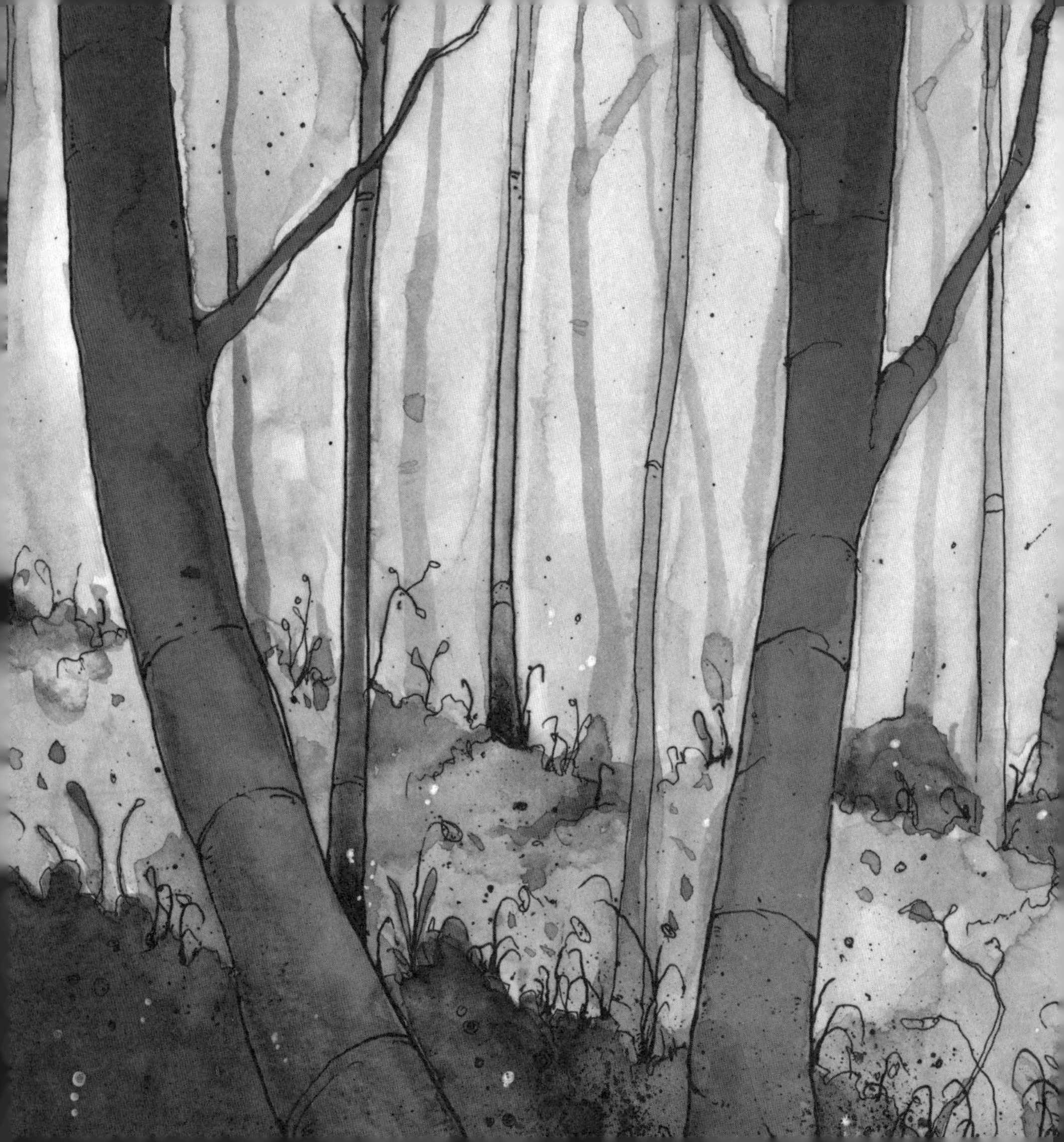

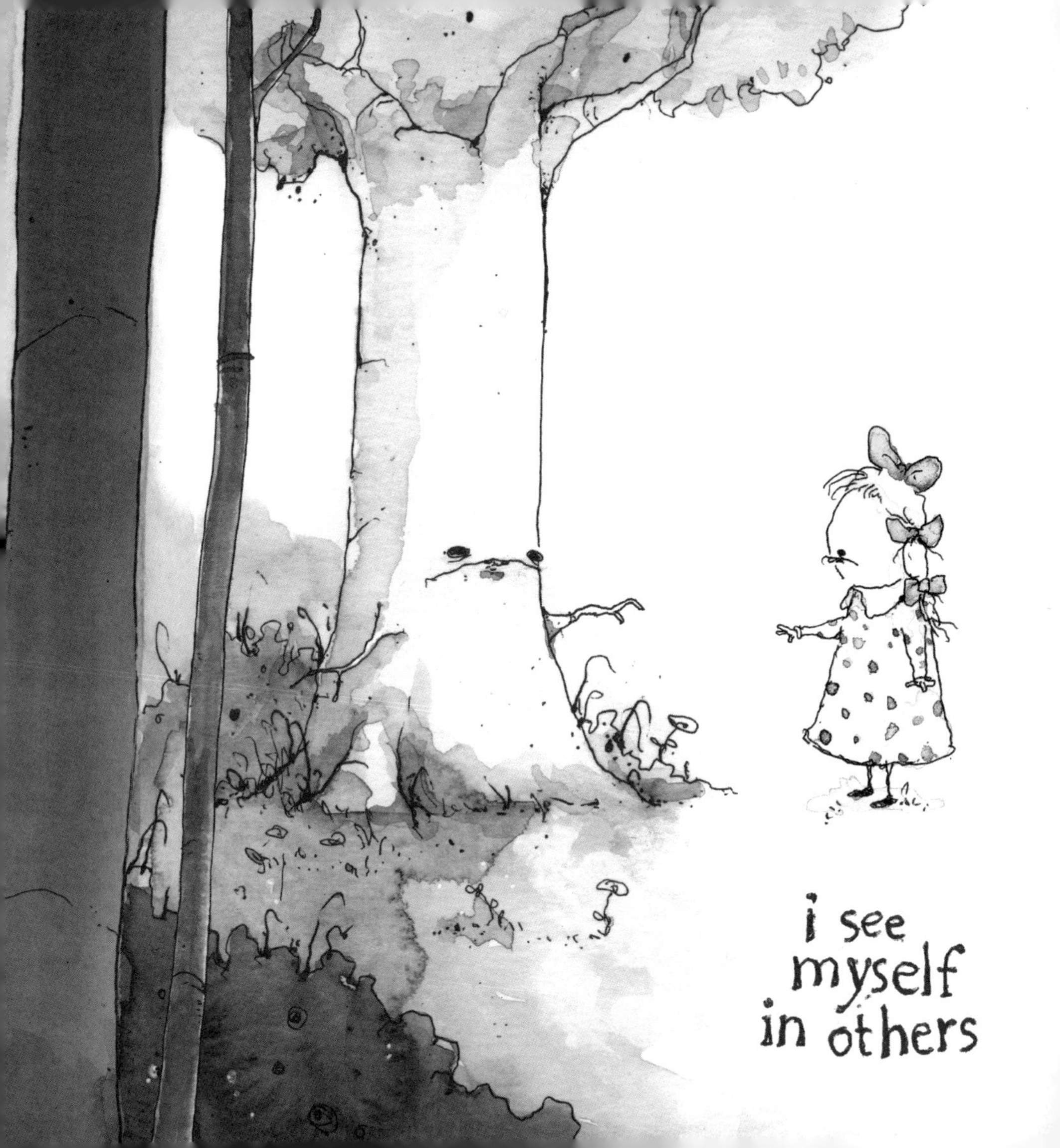

i see
myself
in others

i have everything i need to succeed

i deserve the best

i make time for
what i love

i love dance

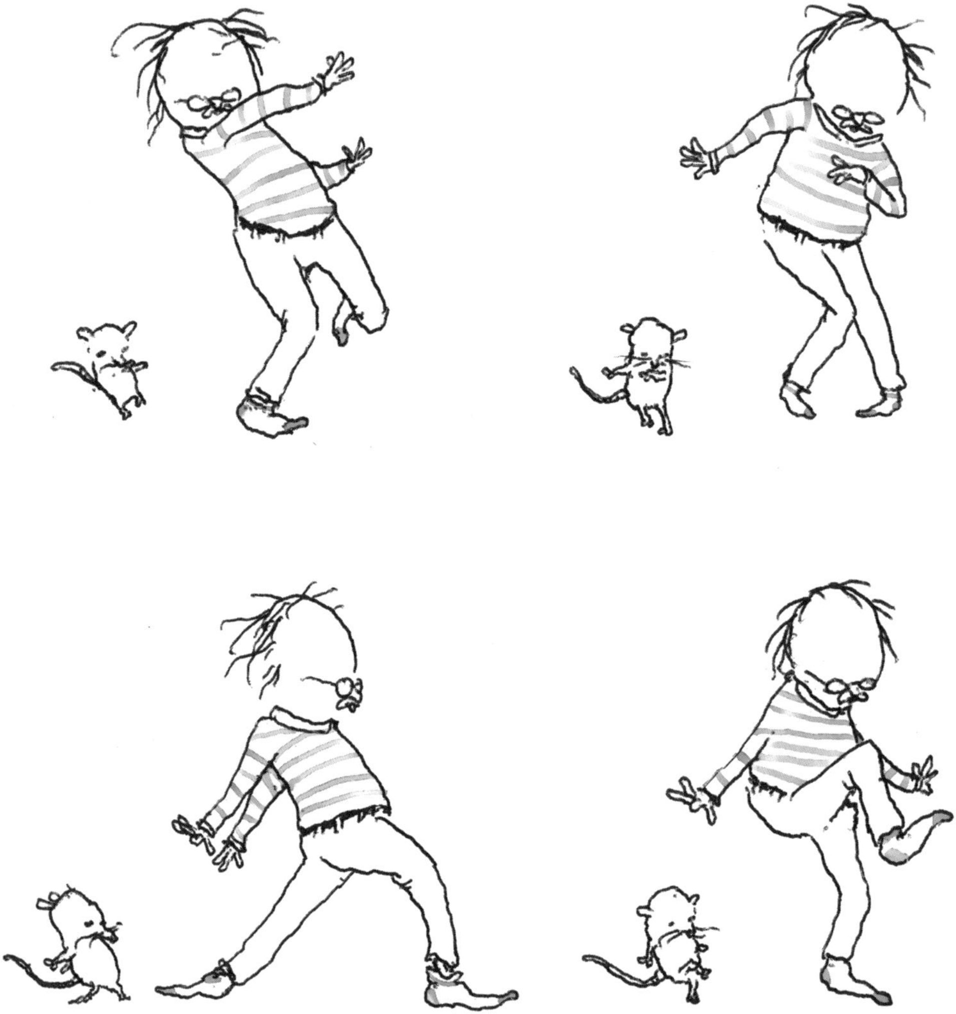

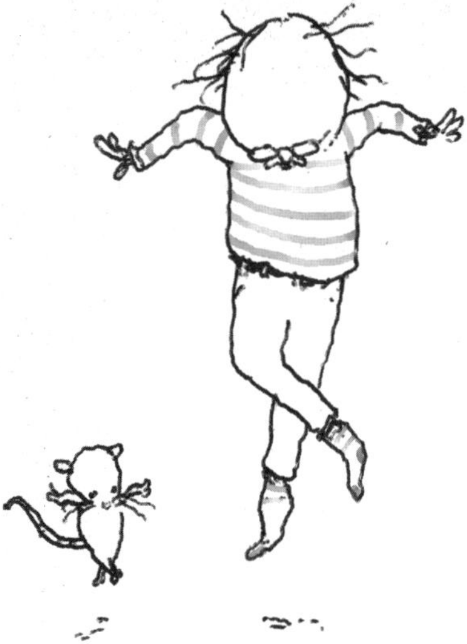
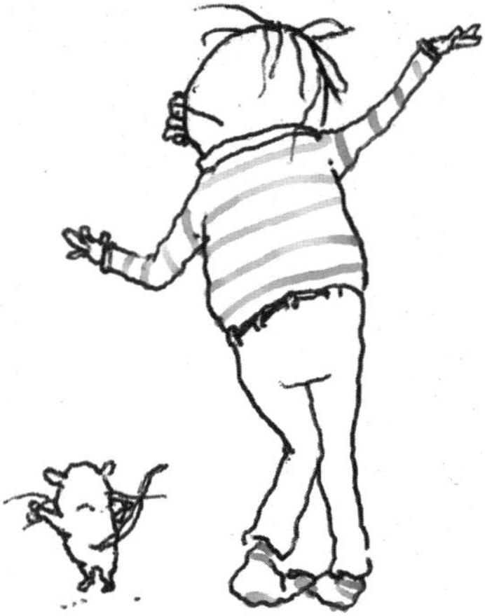
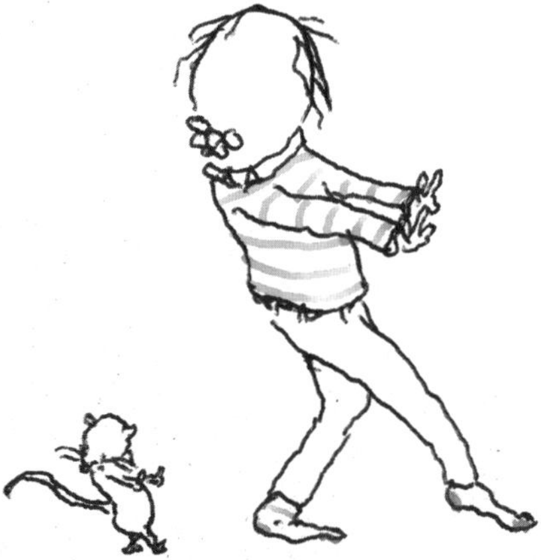
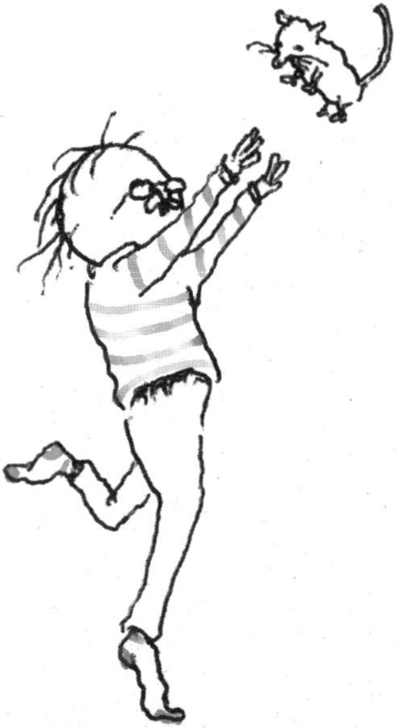

i allow
myself to
slow down

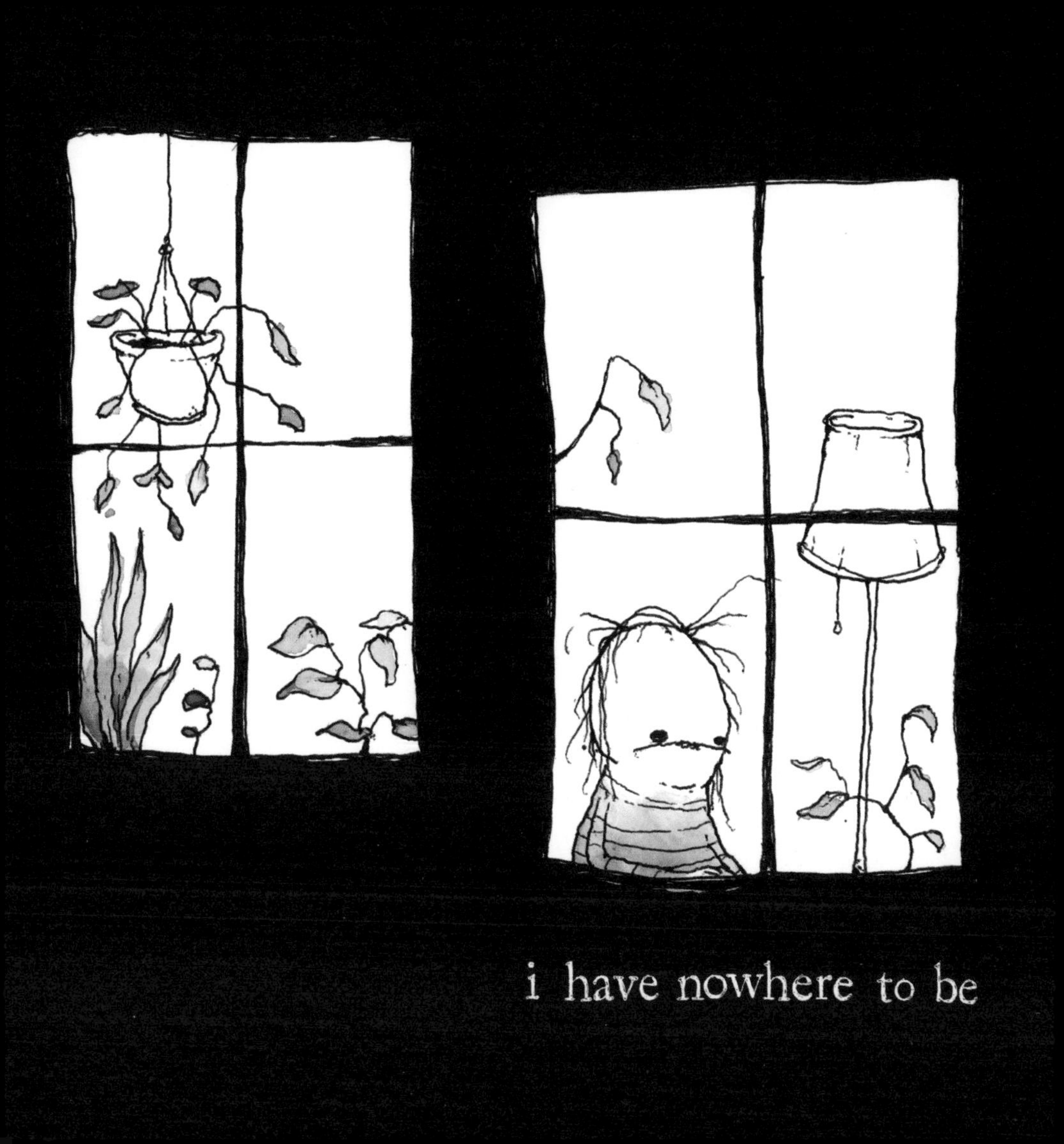
i have nowhere to be

i give the voices
in my head
space to speak

i listen without judgment

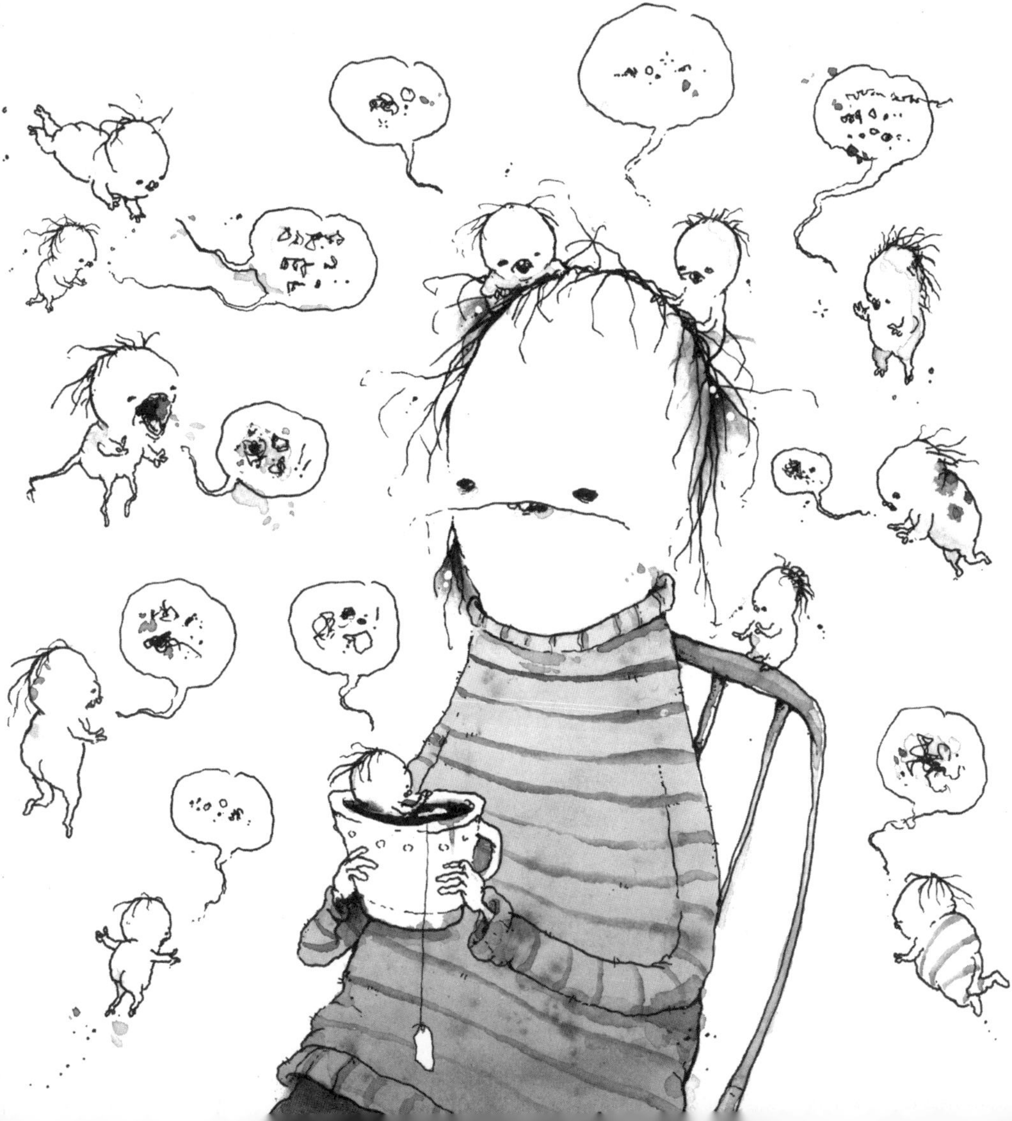

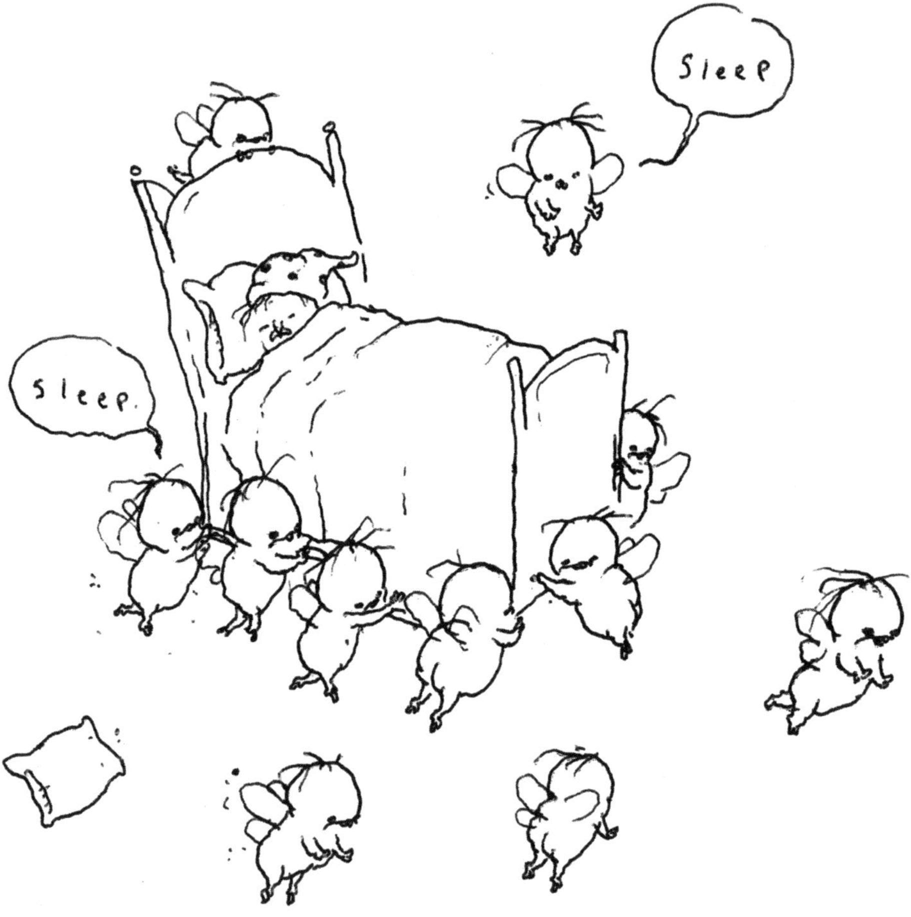
Sleep
Sleep.

i am capable of falling asleep

sleep comes
naturally
to me

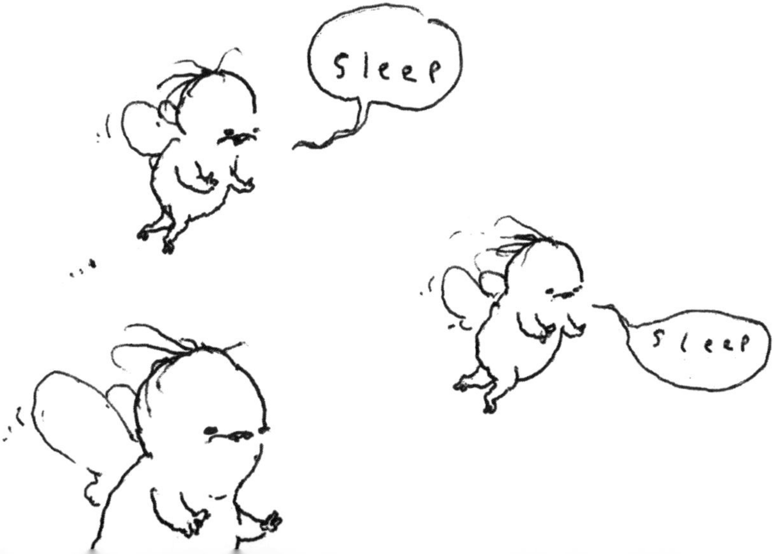
sleep
sleep

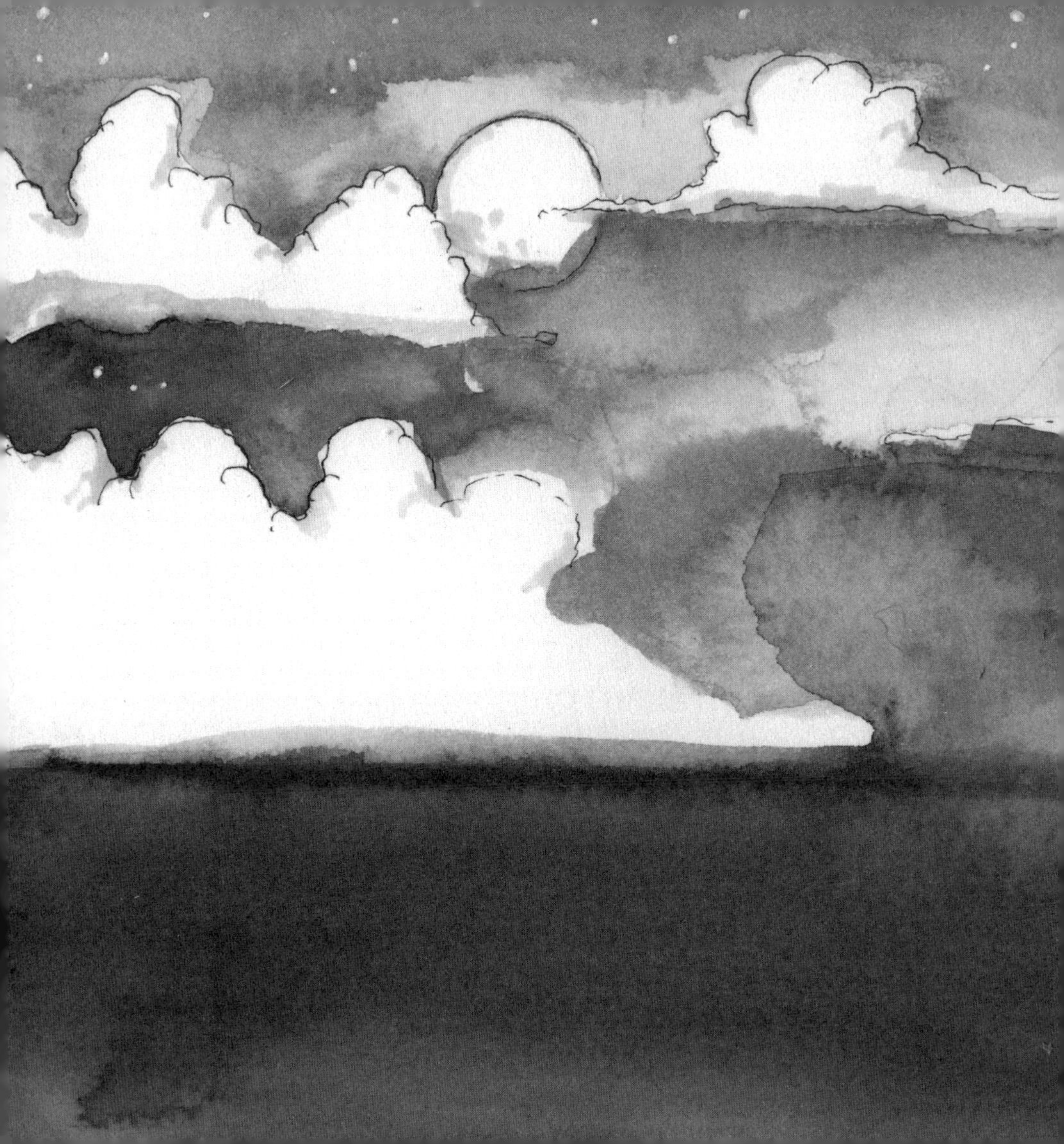

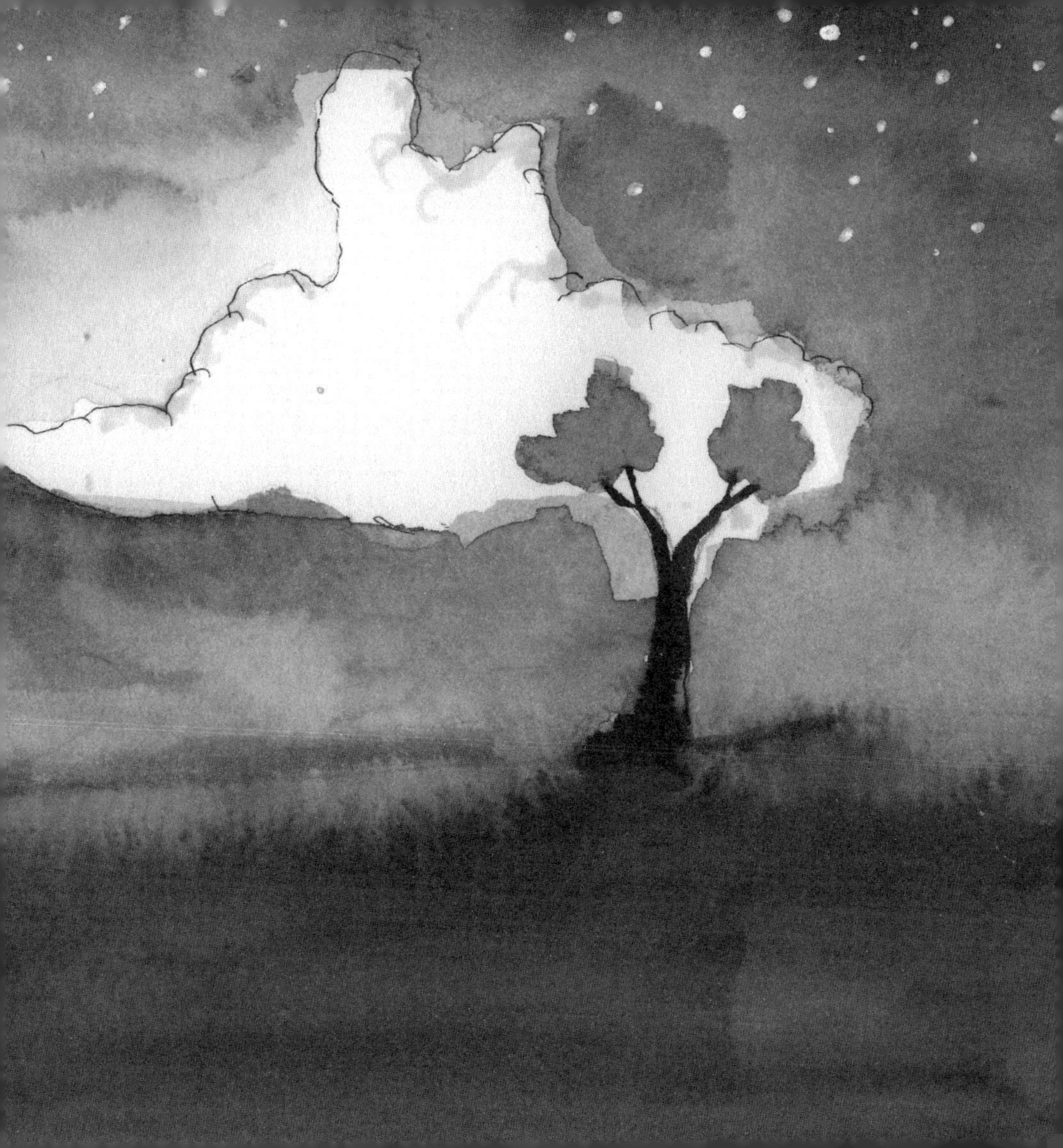

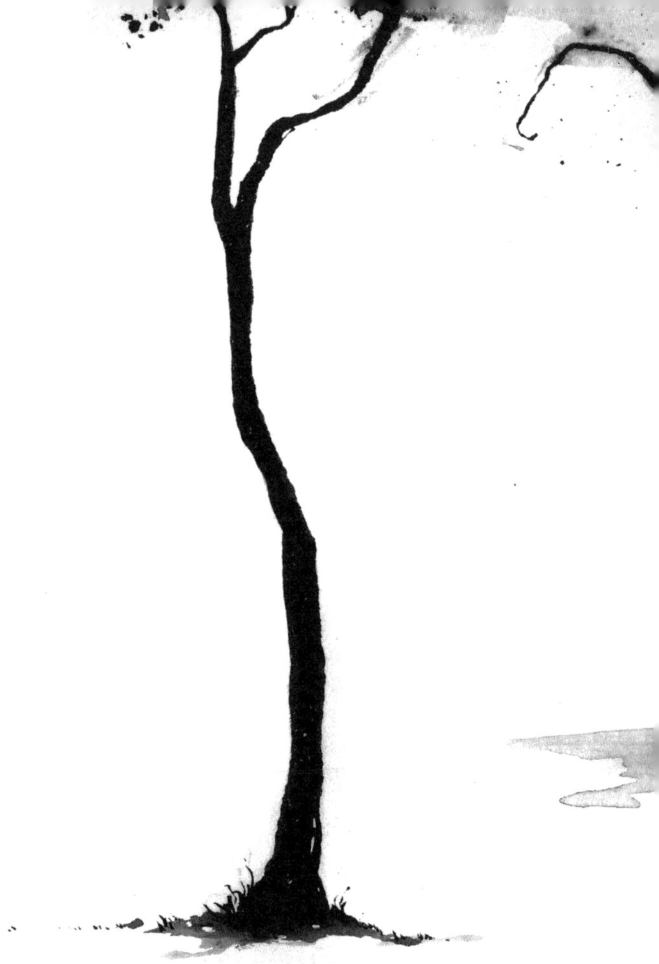

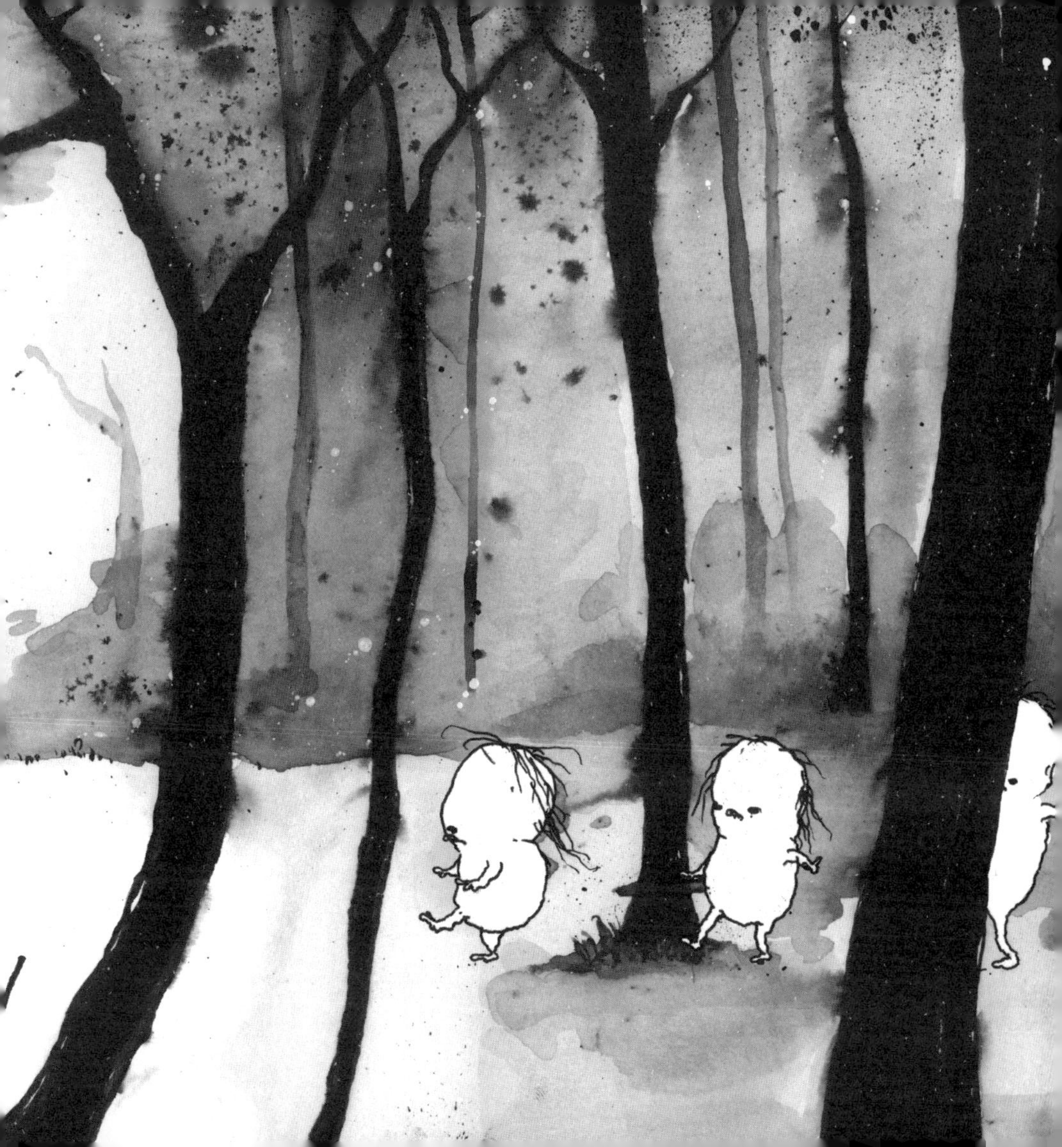

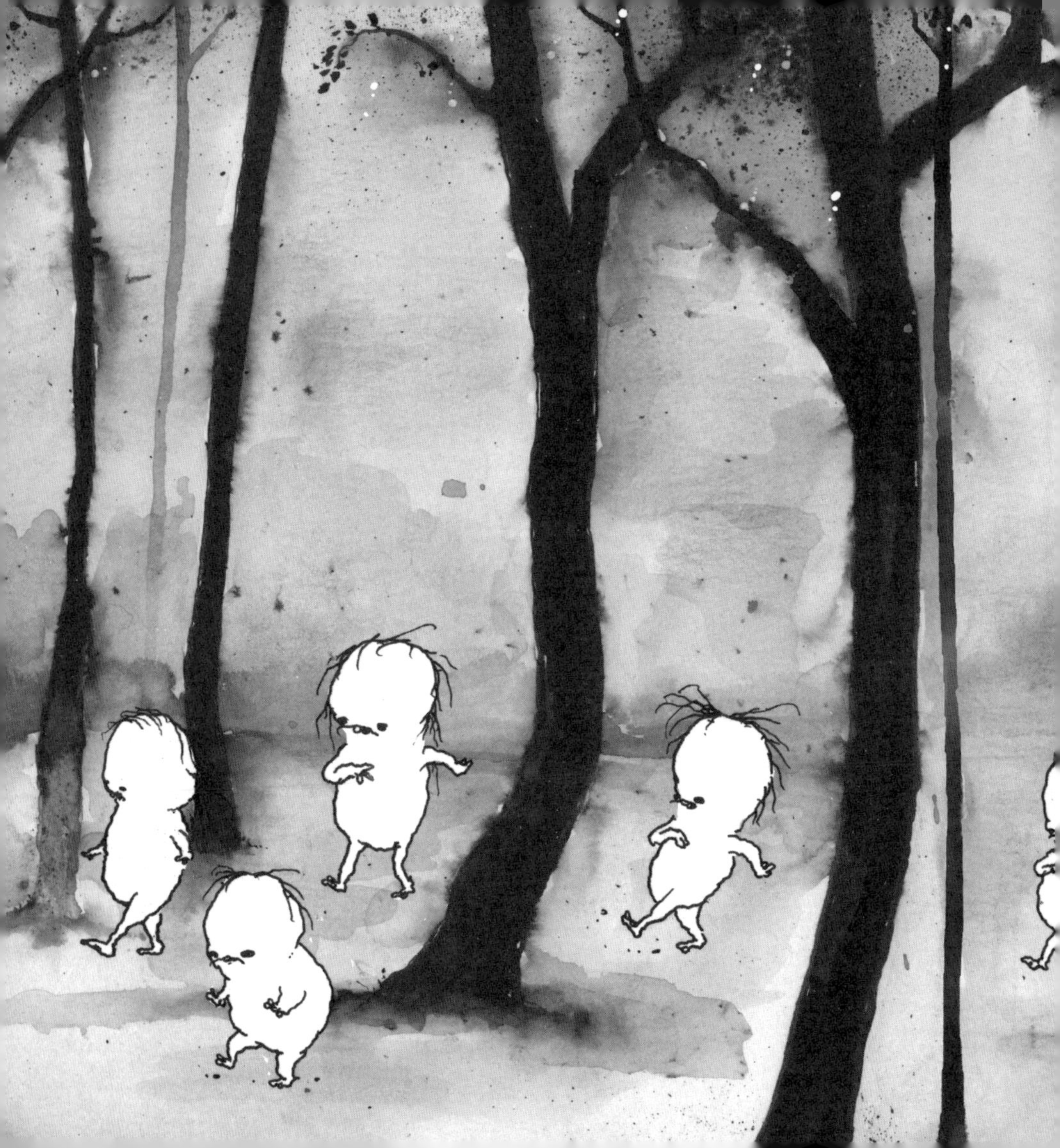

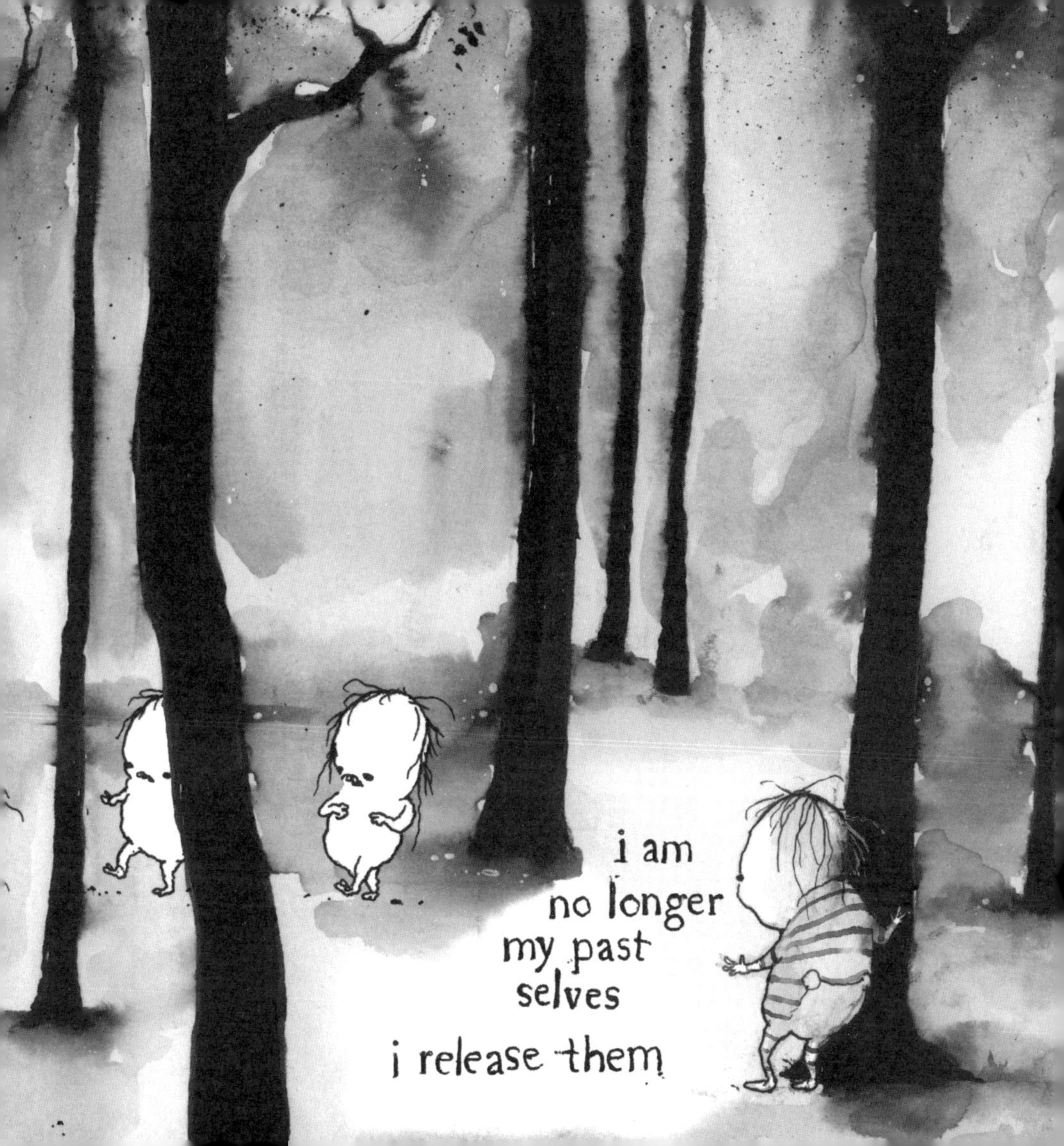
i am
no longer
my past
selves
i release them

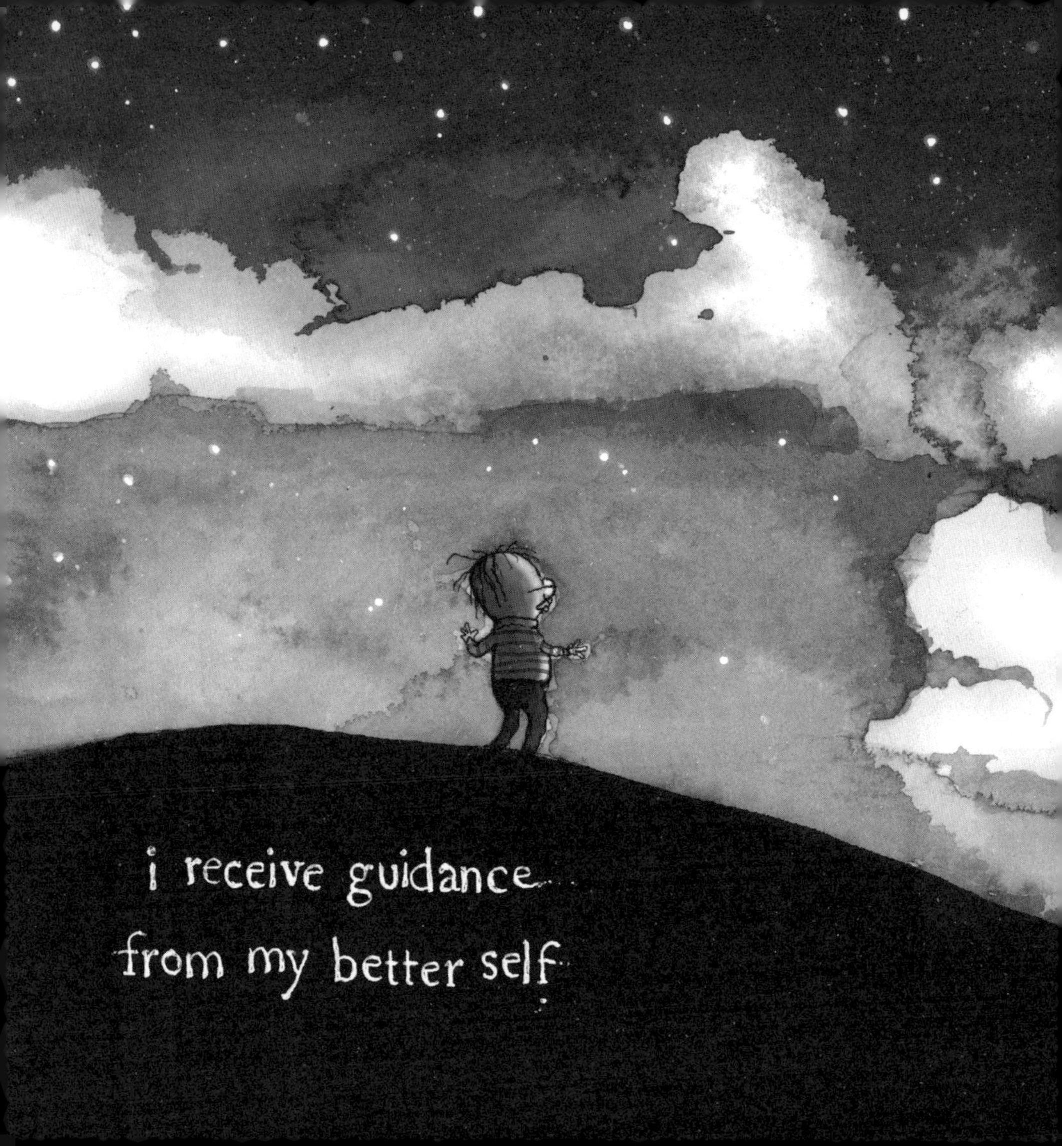
i receive guidance...
from my better self.

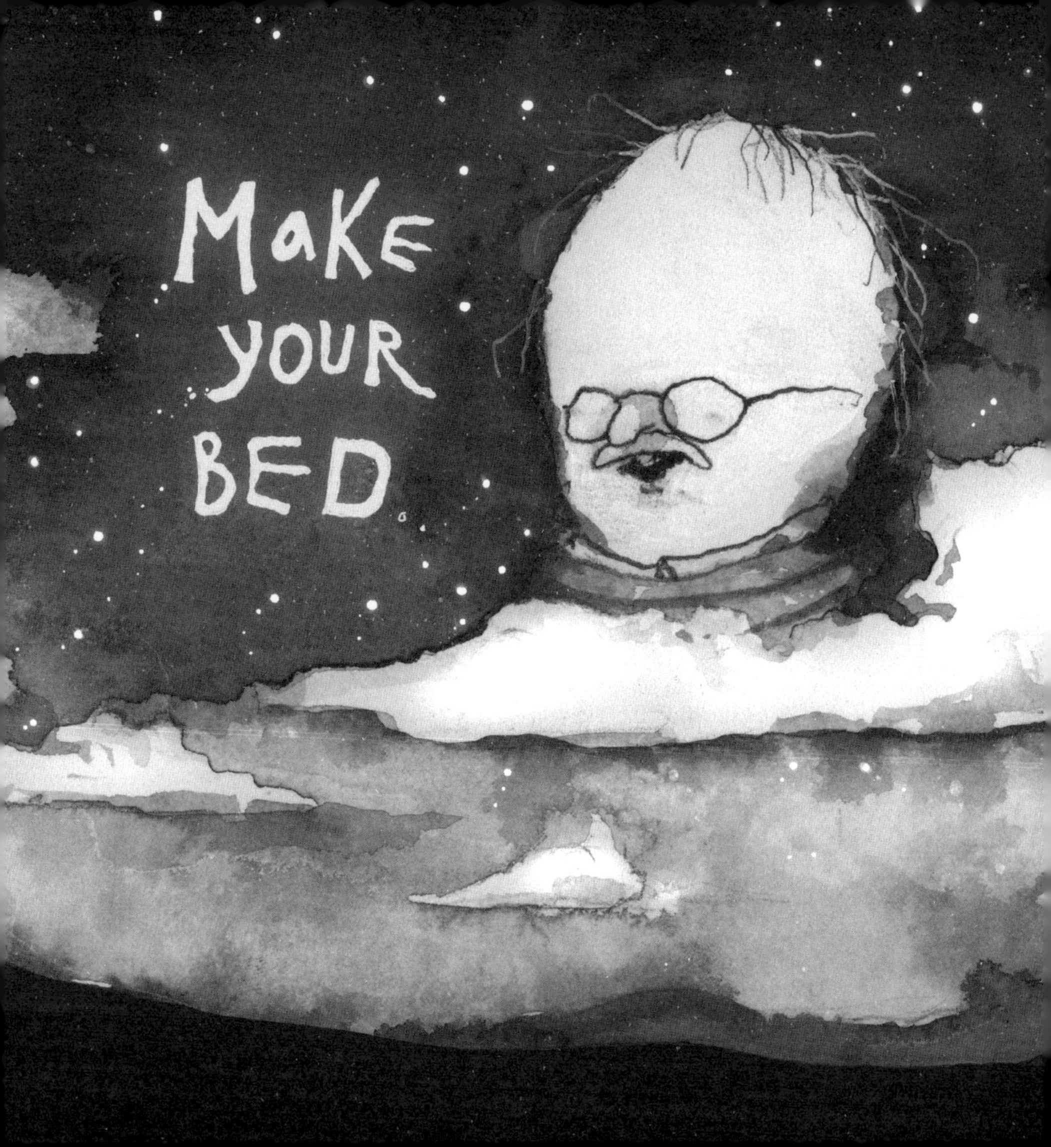
MAKE YOUR BED

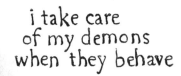

i take care
of my demons
when they behave

i bring my
demons treats

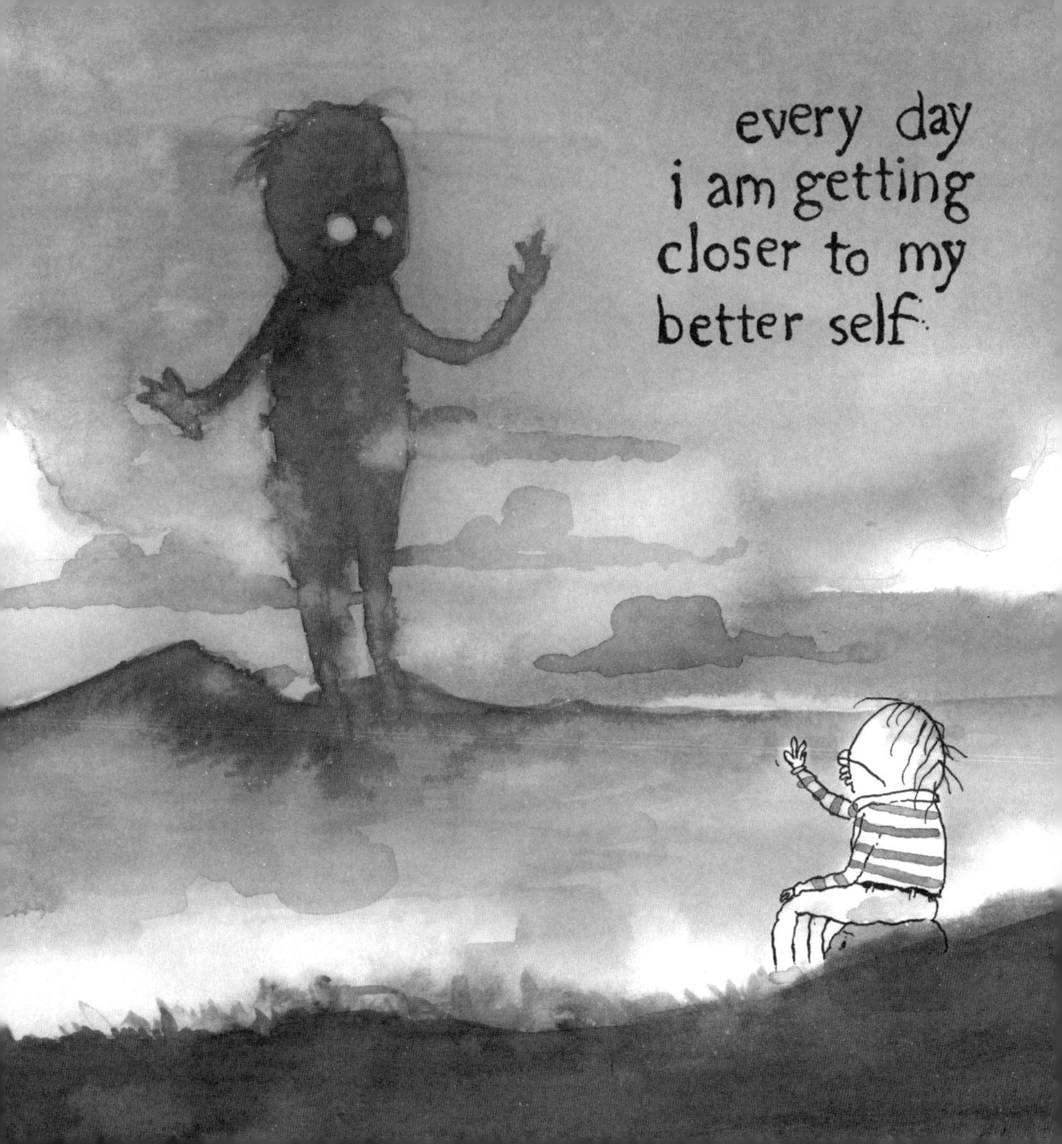
every day
i am getting
closer to my
better self

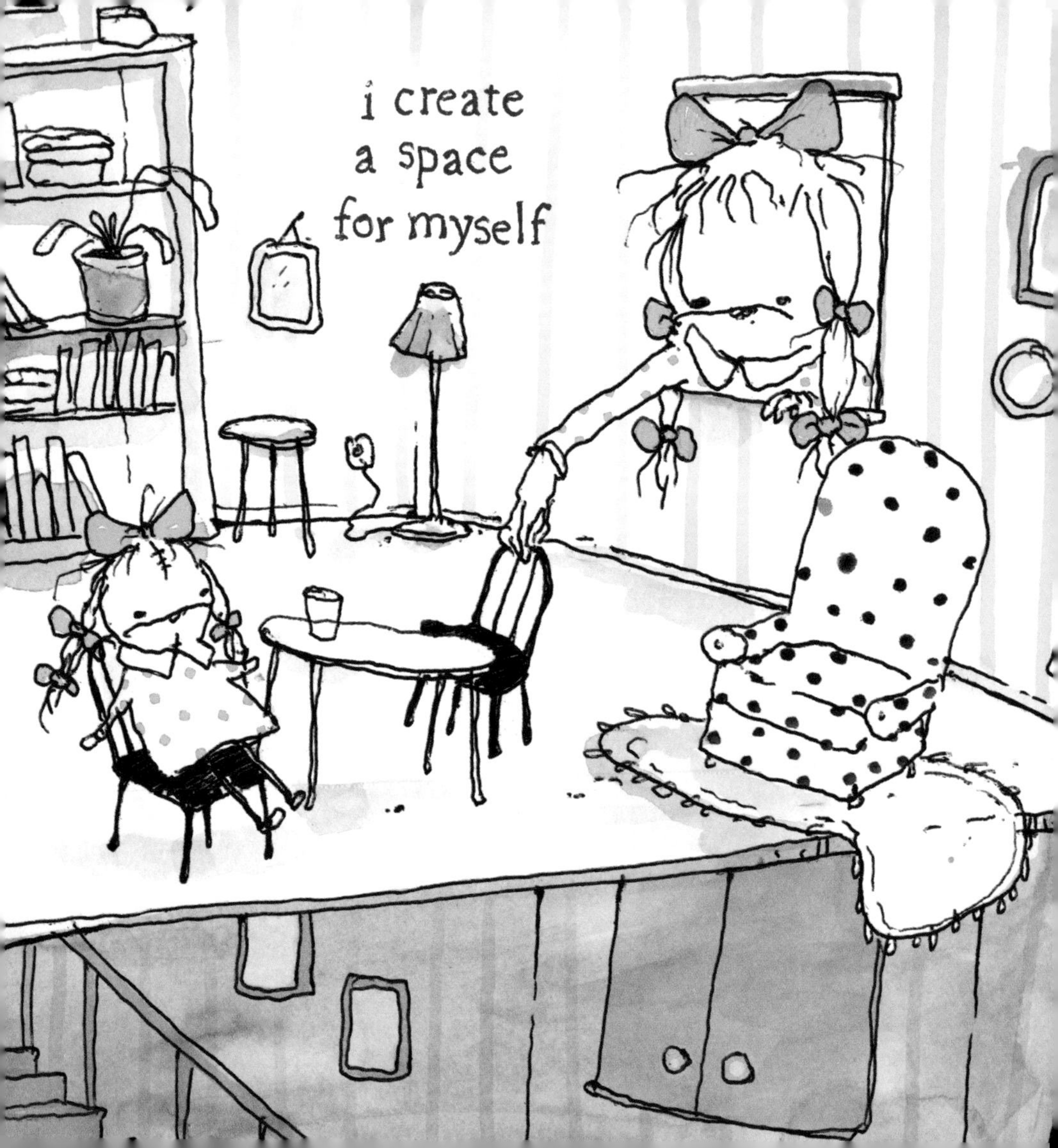
i create
a space
for myself

i let my inner guide
take me where
i need to go

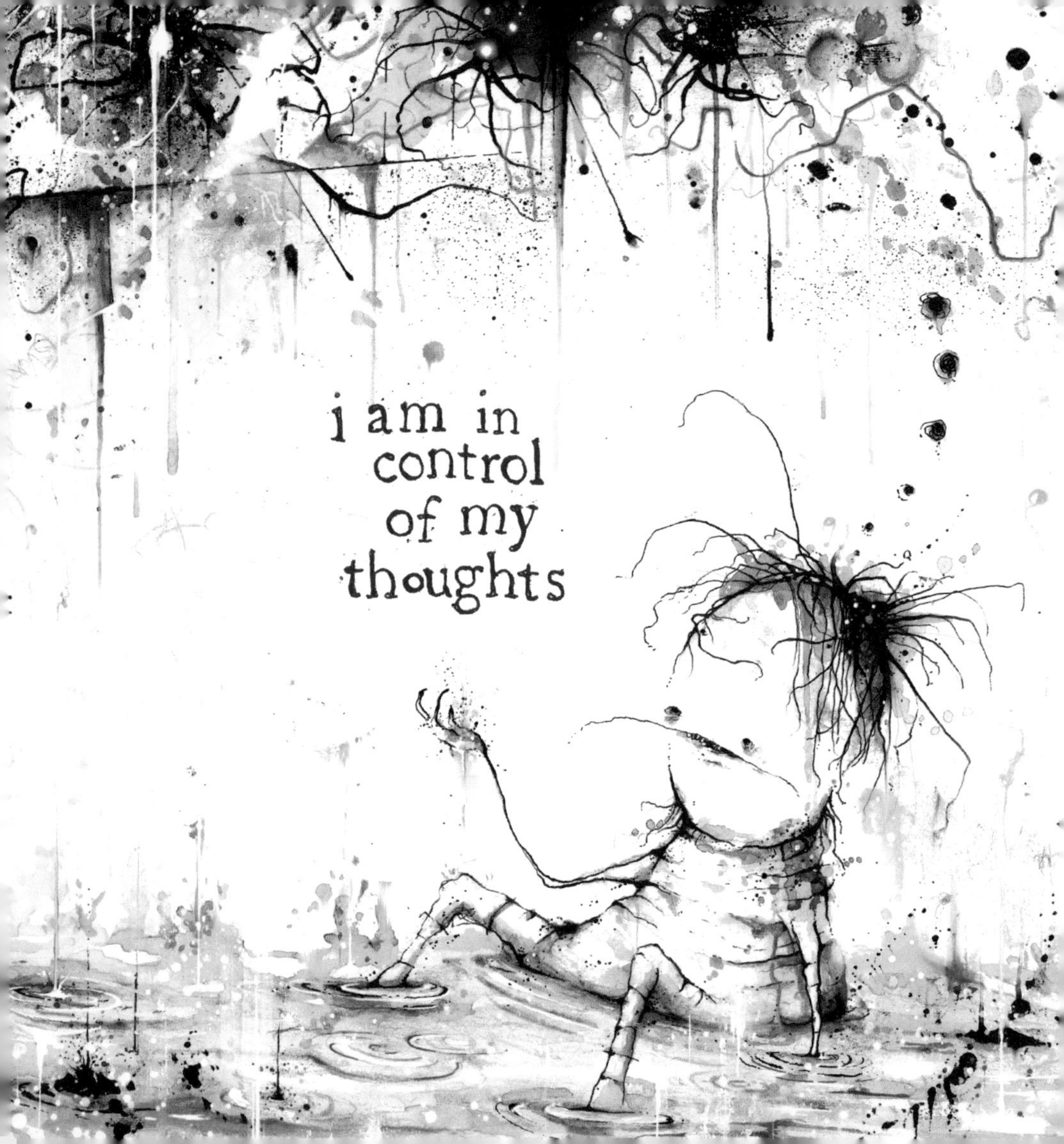
i am in
control
of my
thoughts

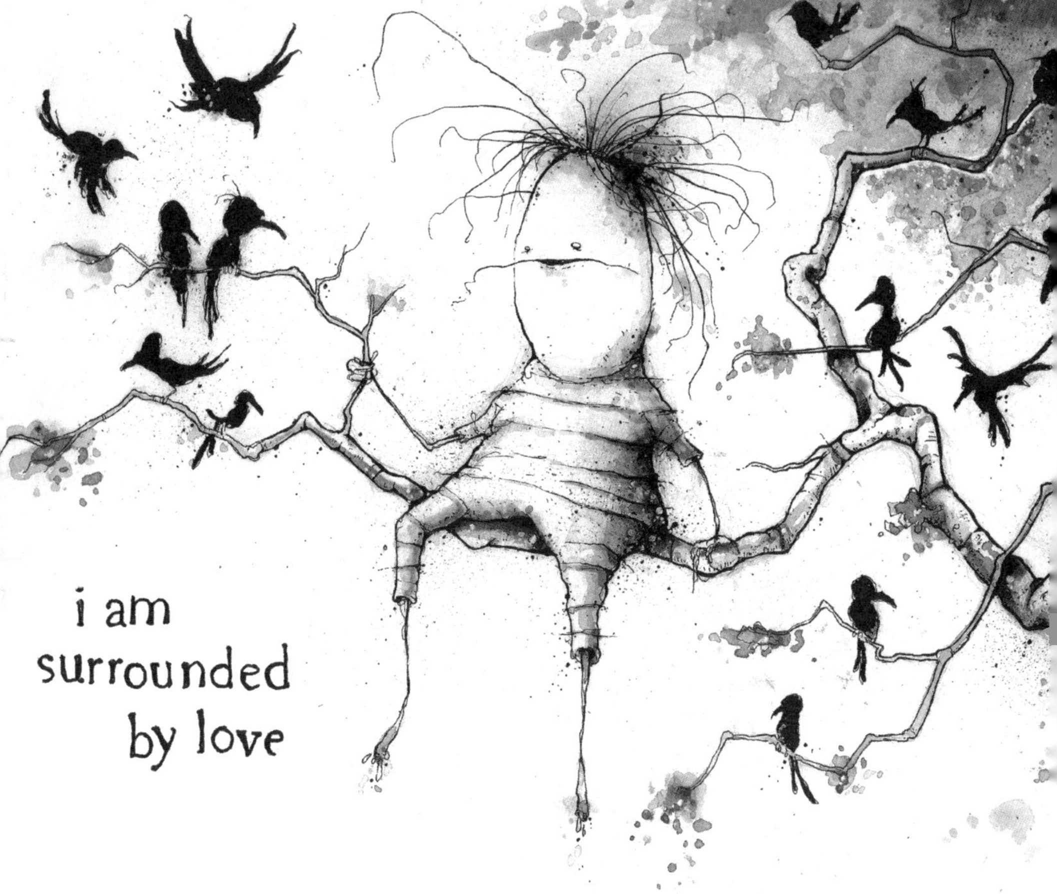

i am
surrounded
by love

i attract happiness
into my life

i am
grateful
for this
moment

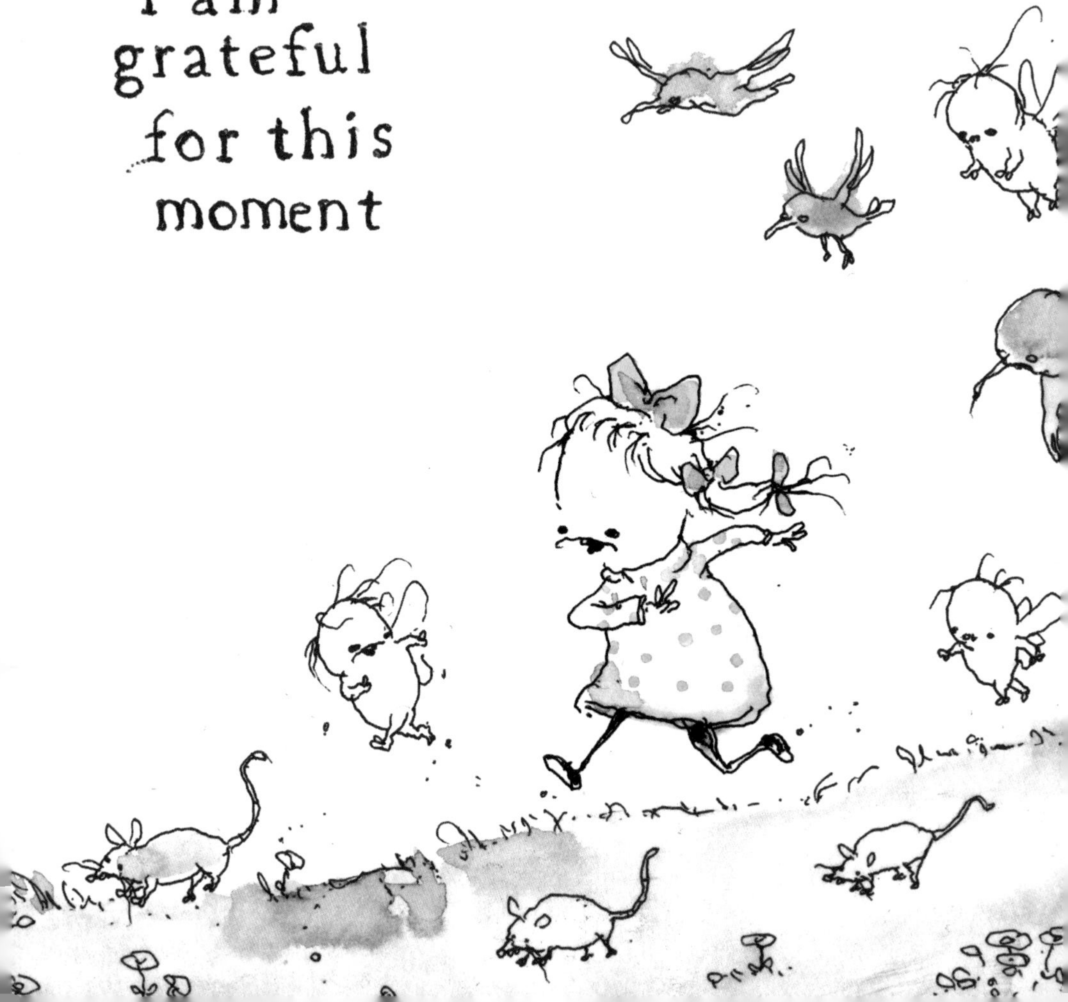

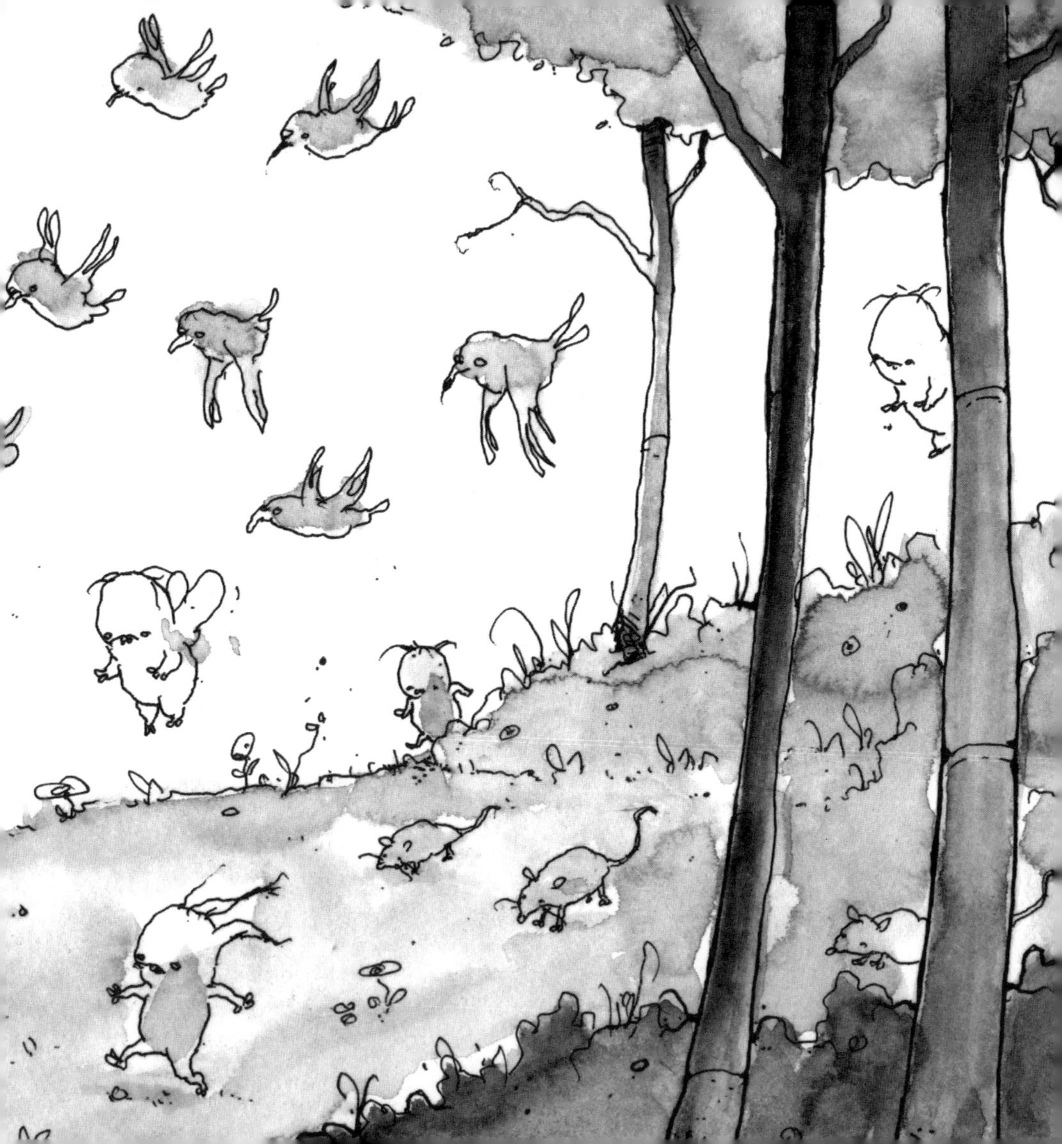

i am filled with
clarity and purpose

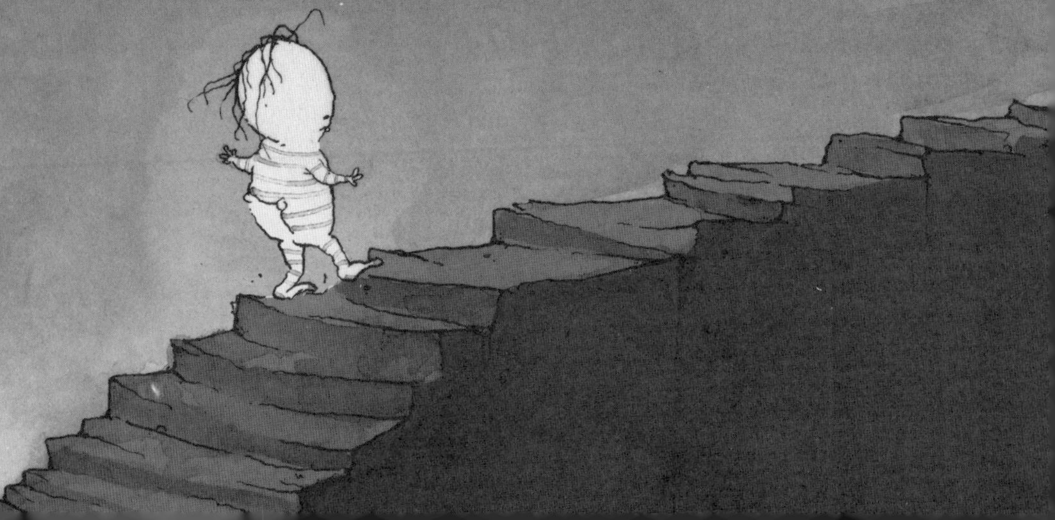

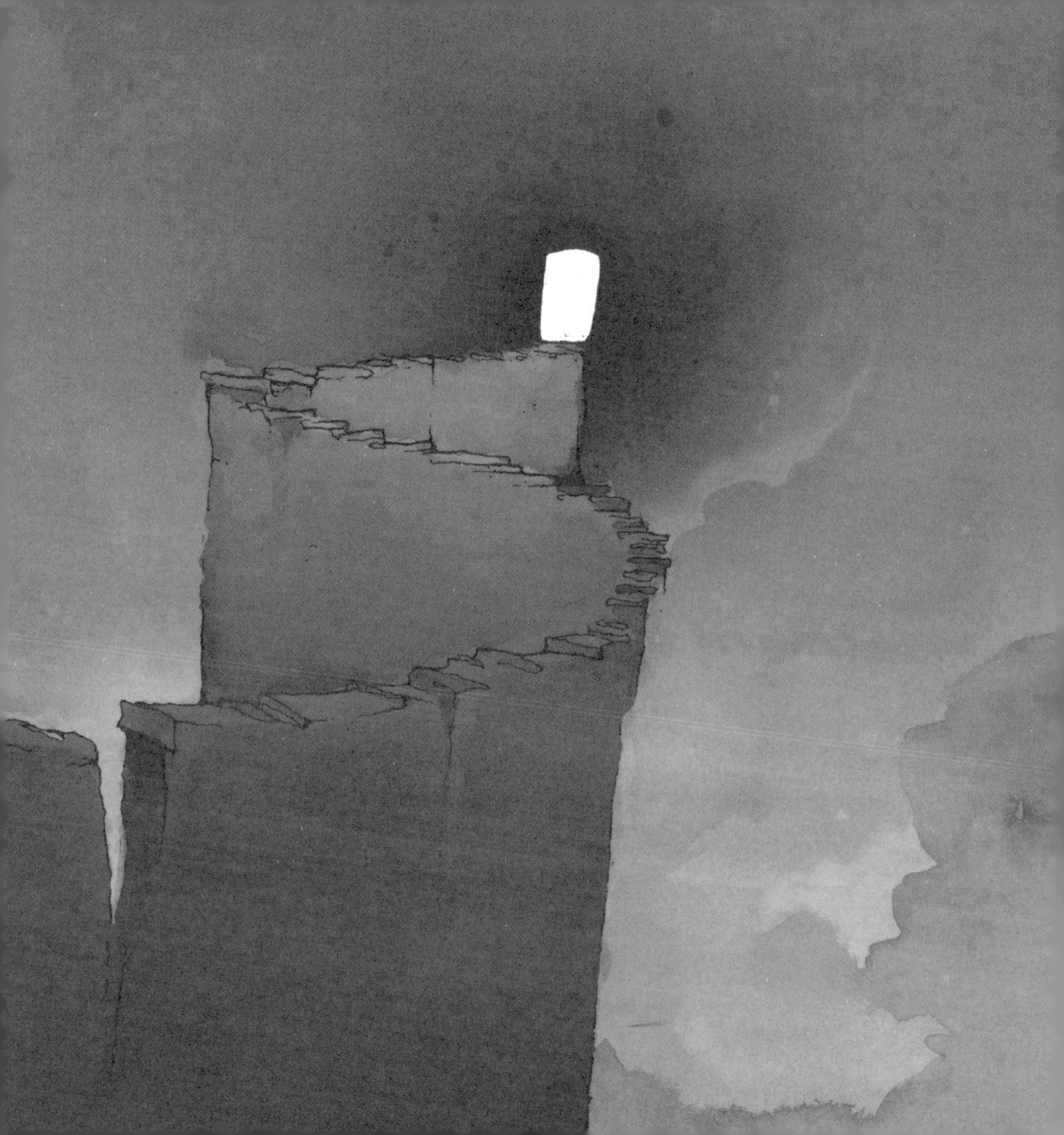

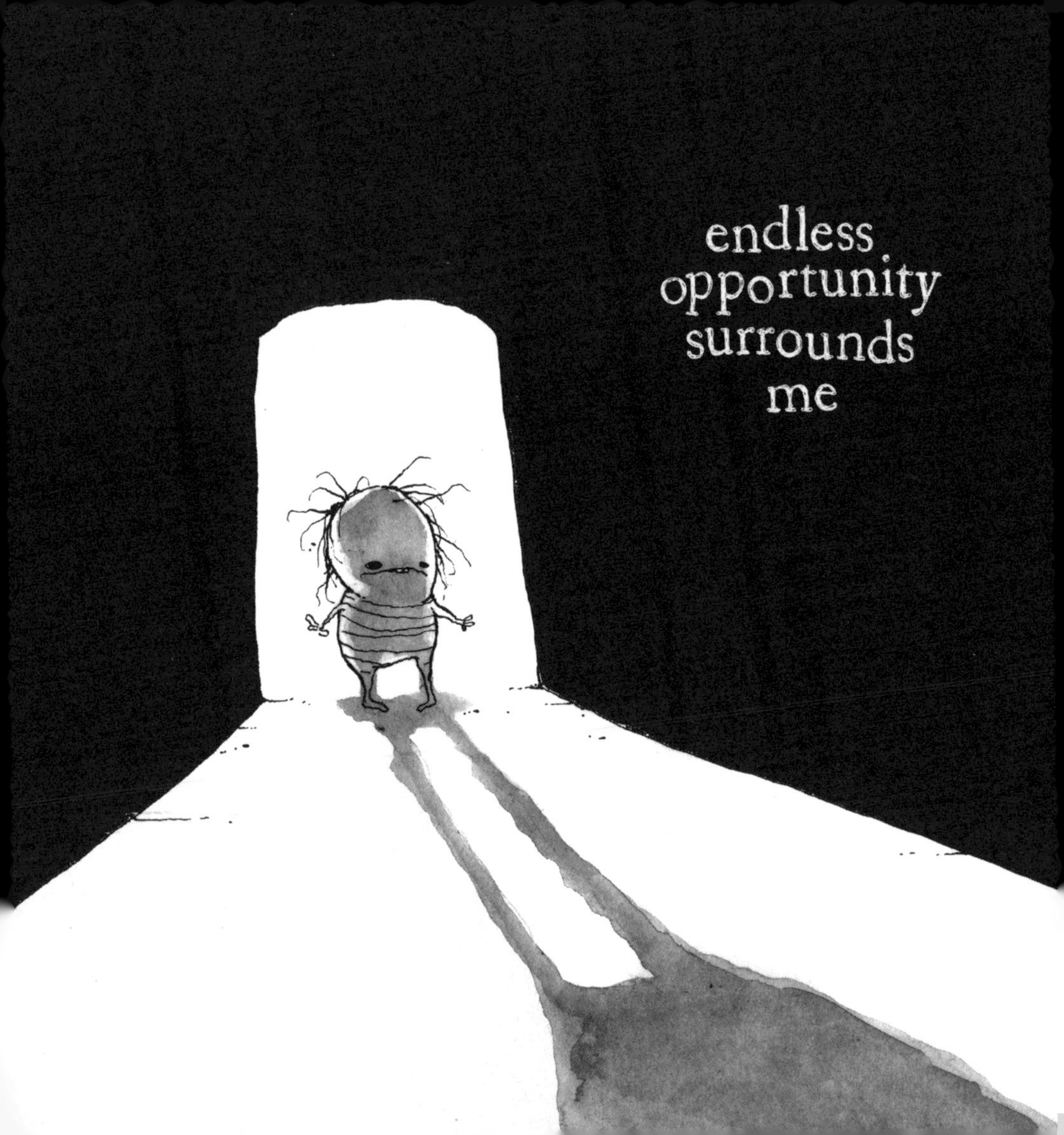
endless
opportunity
surrounds
me

new doors are
opening

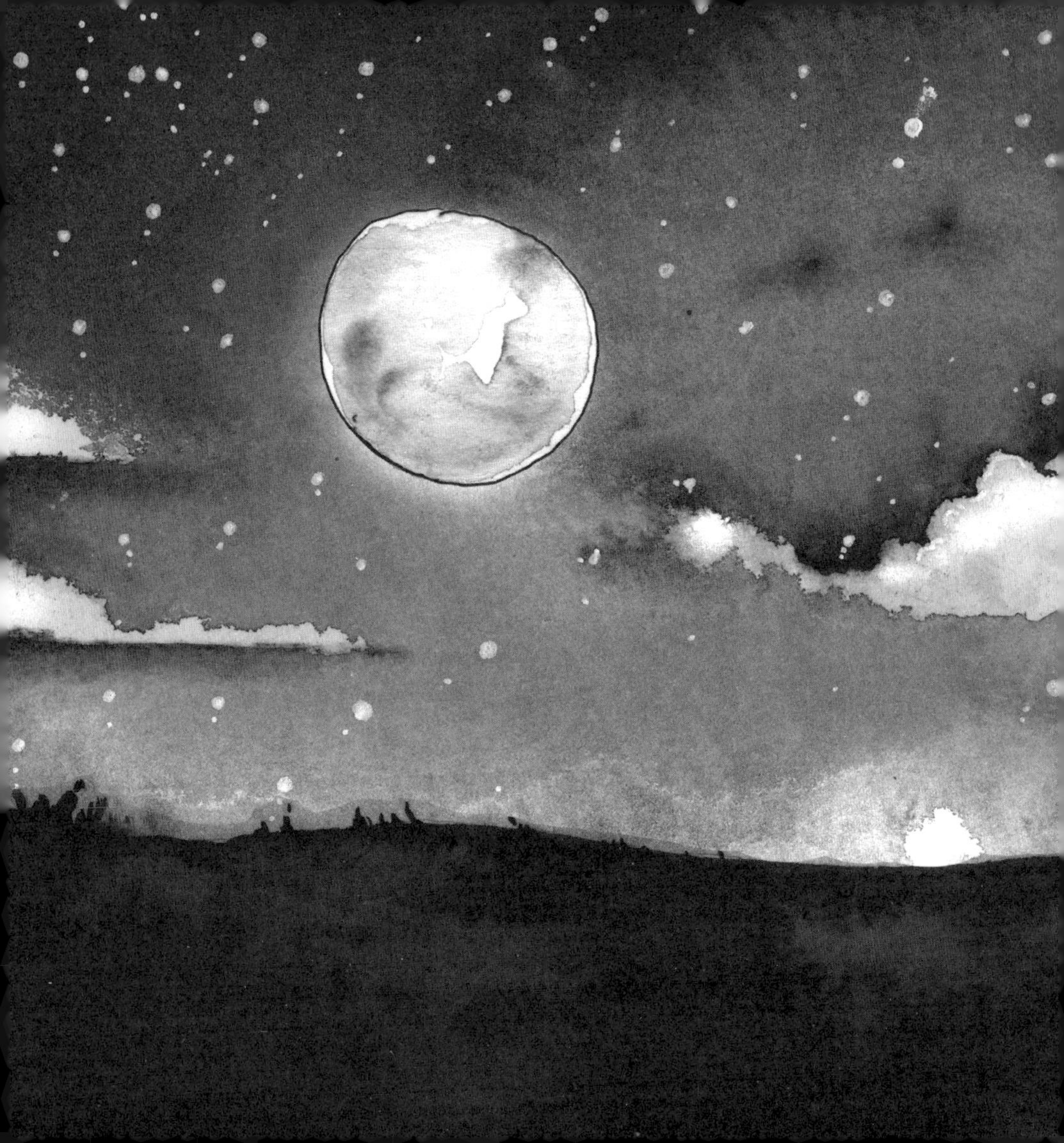

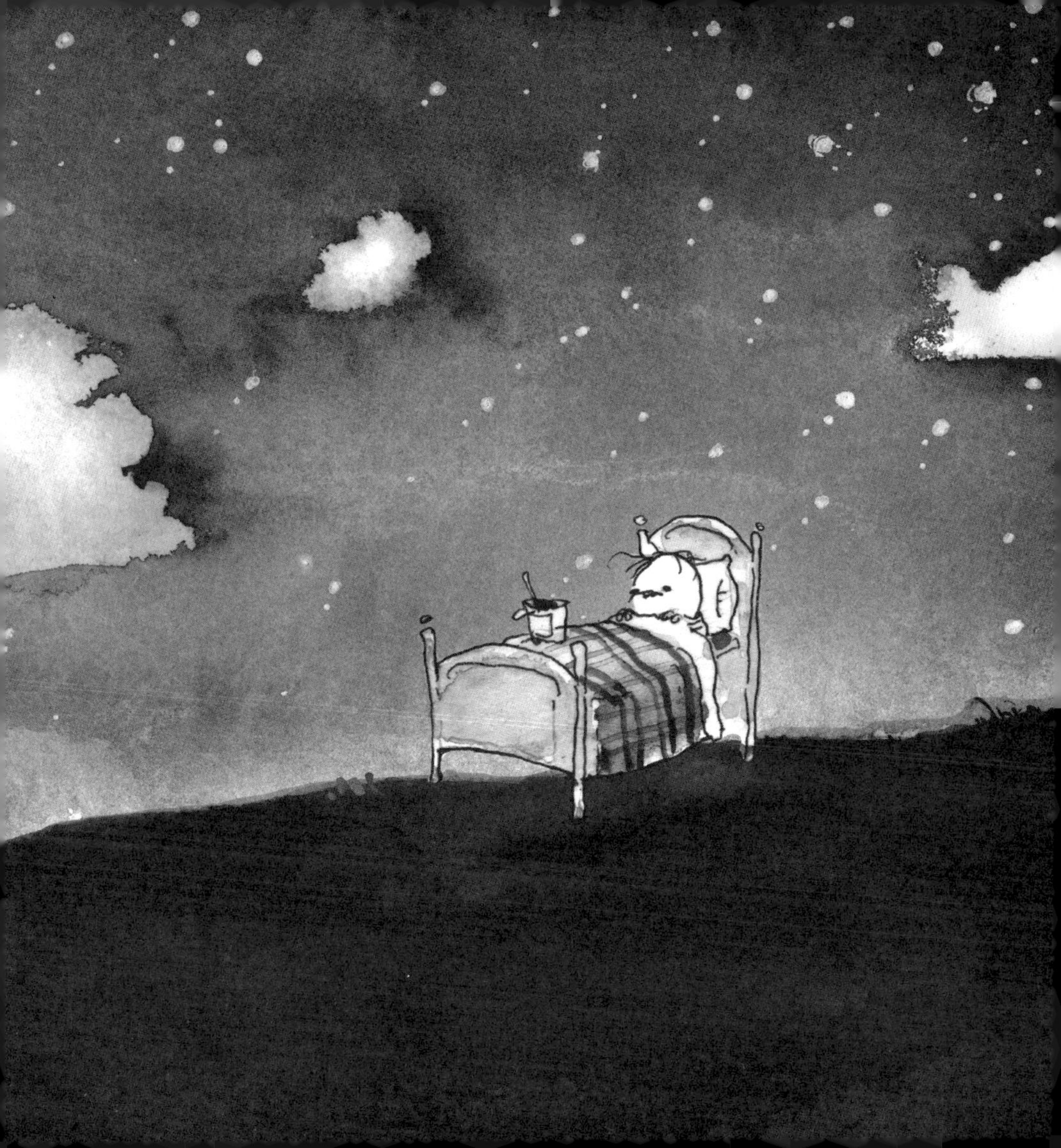

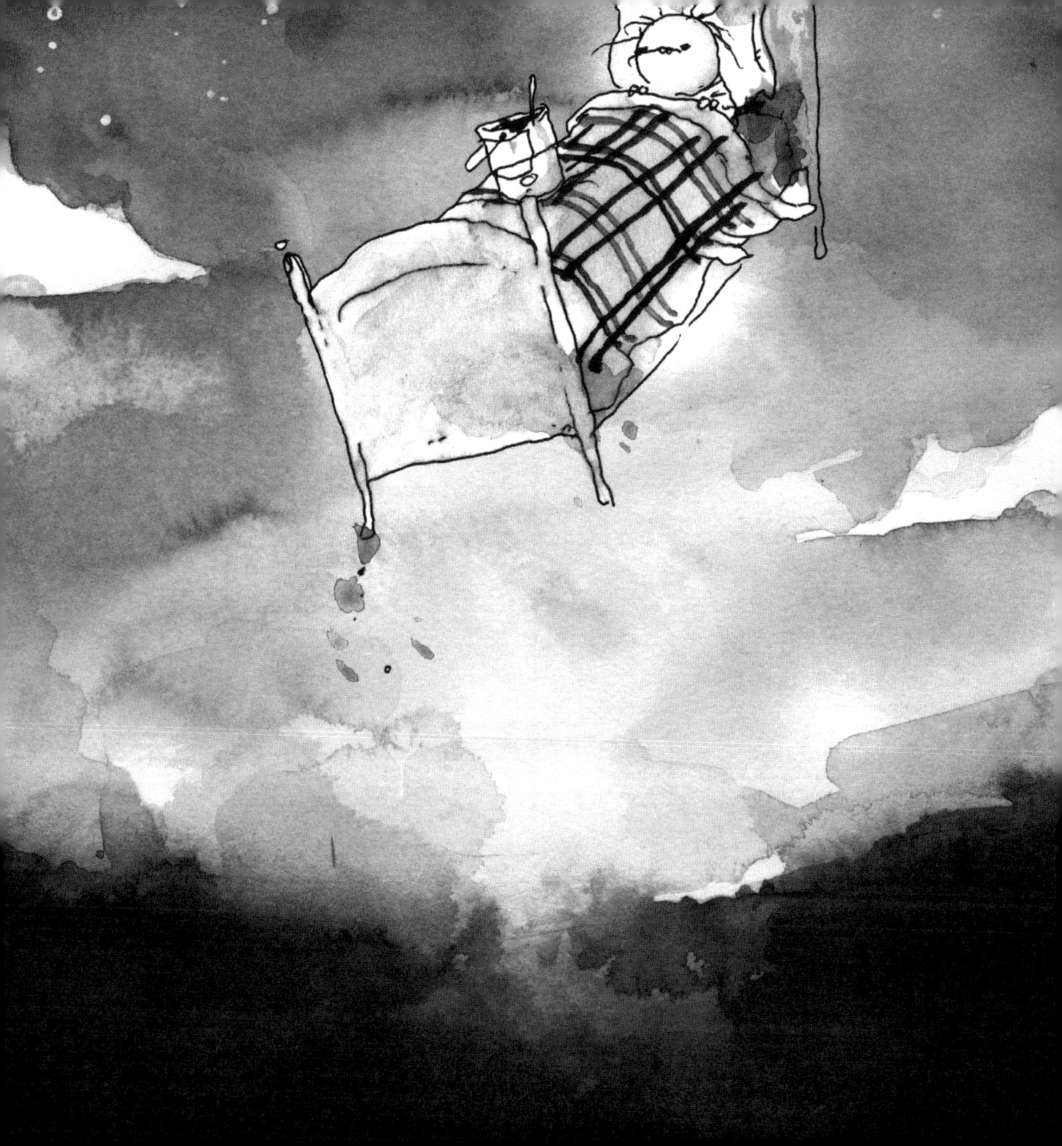

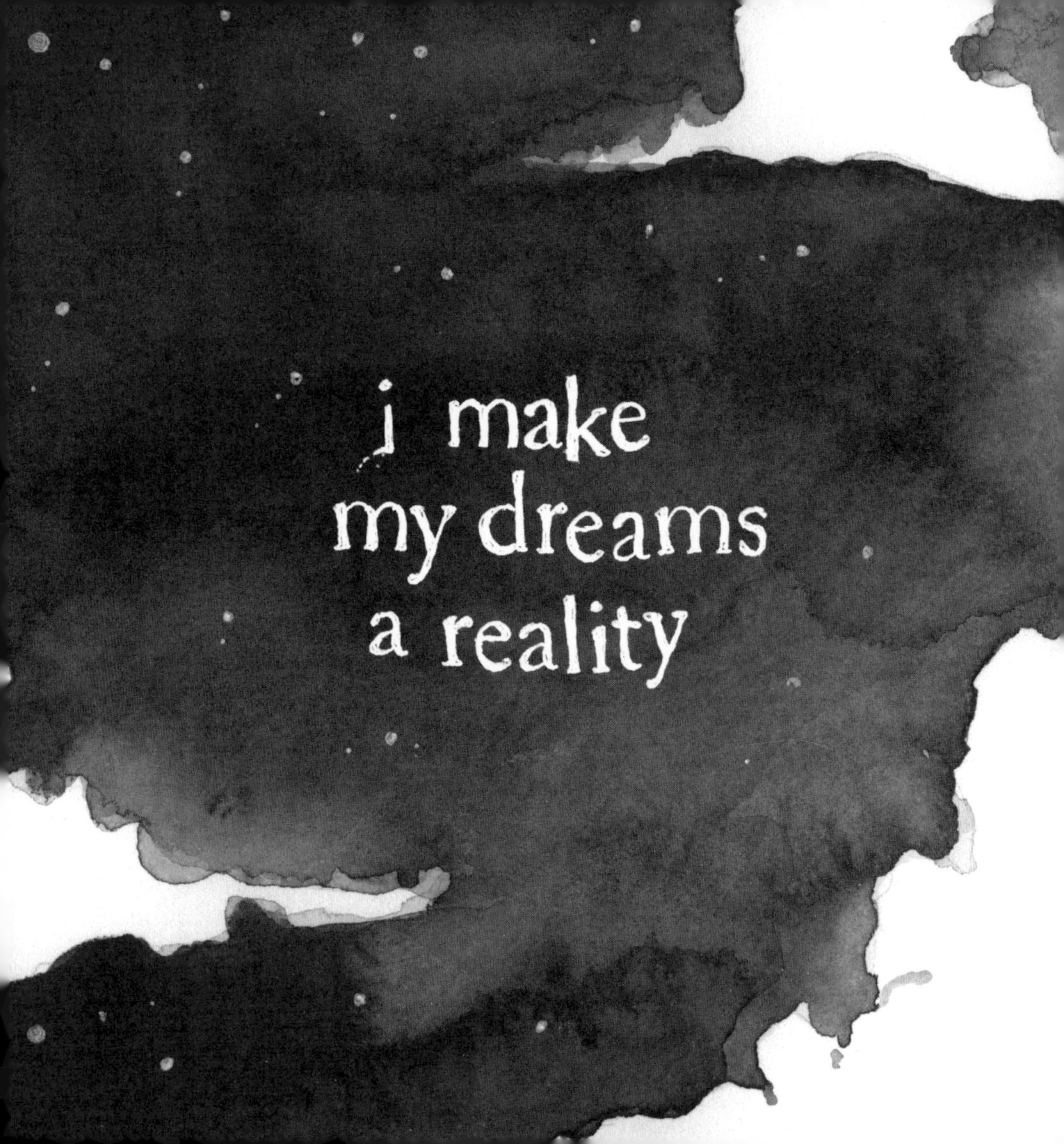
i make
my dreams
a reality

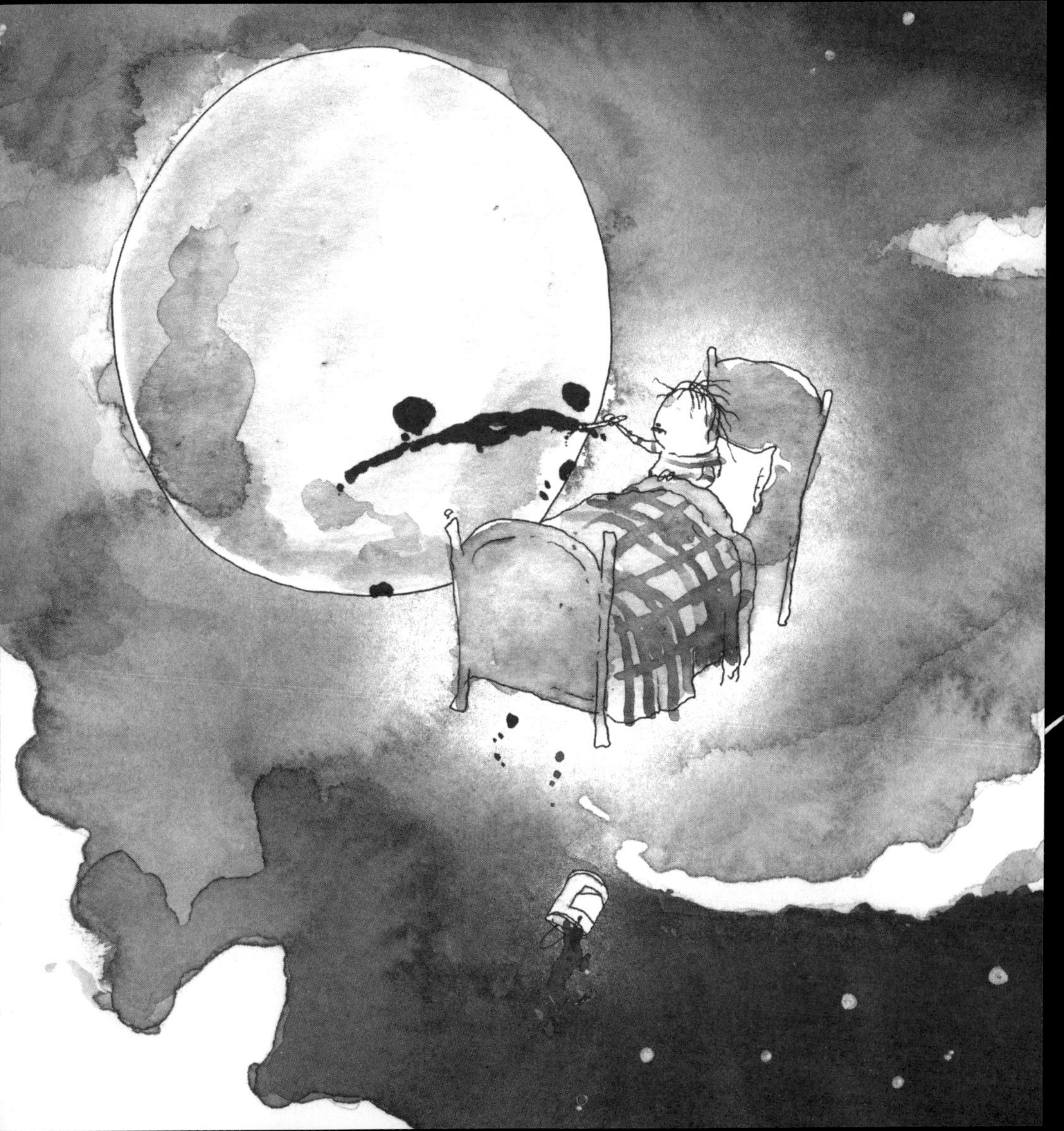

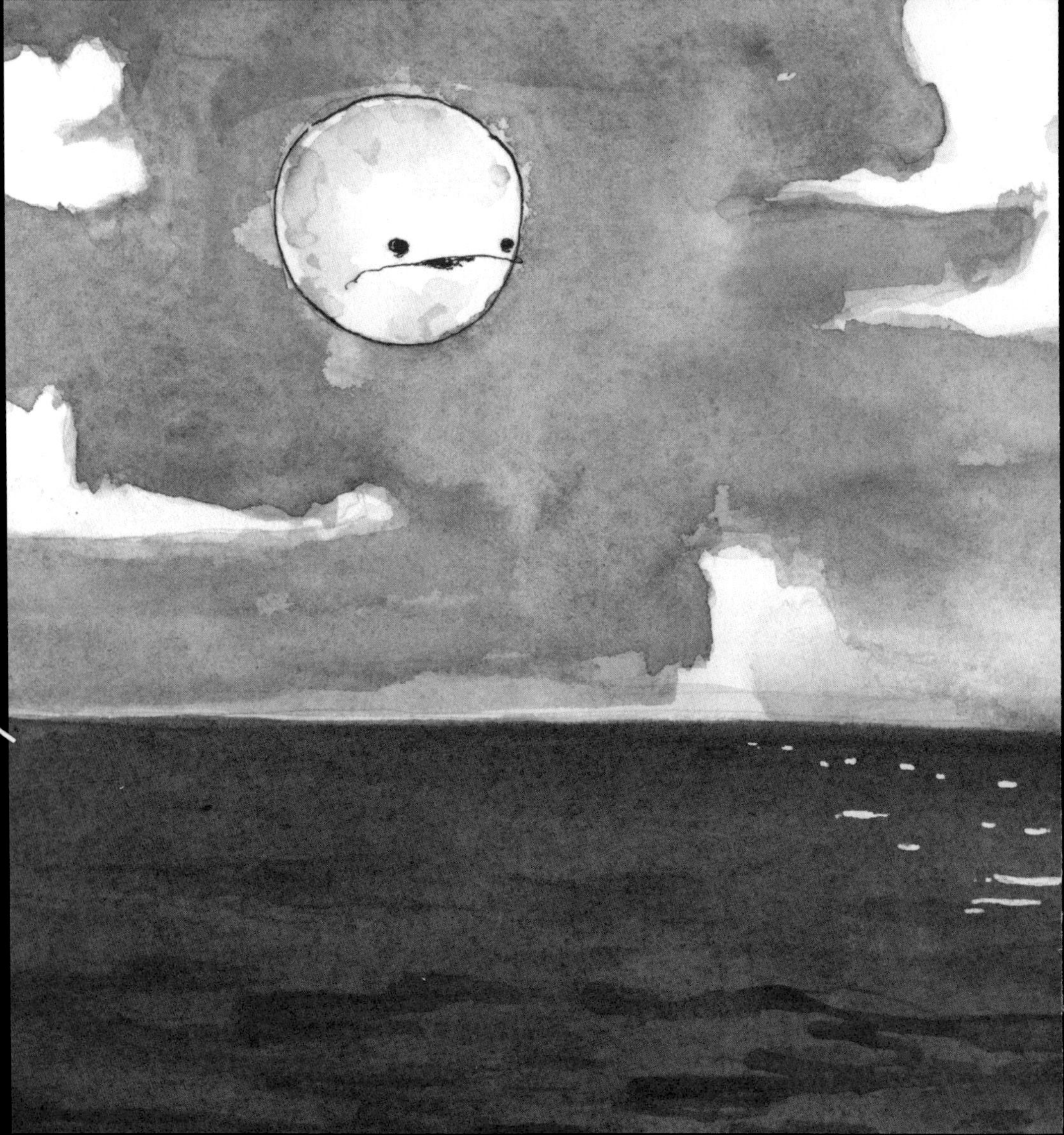

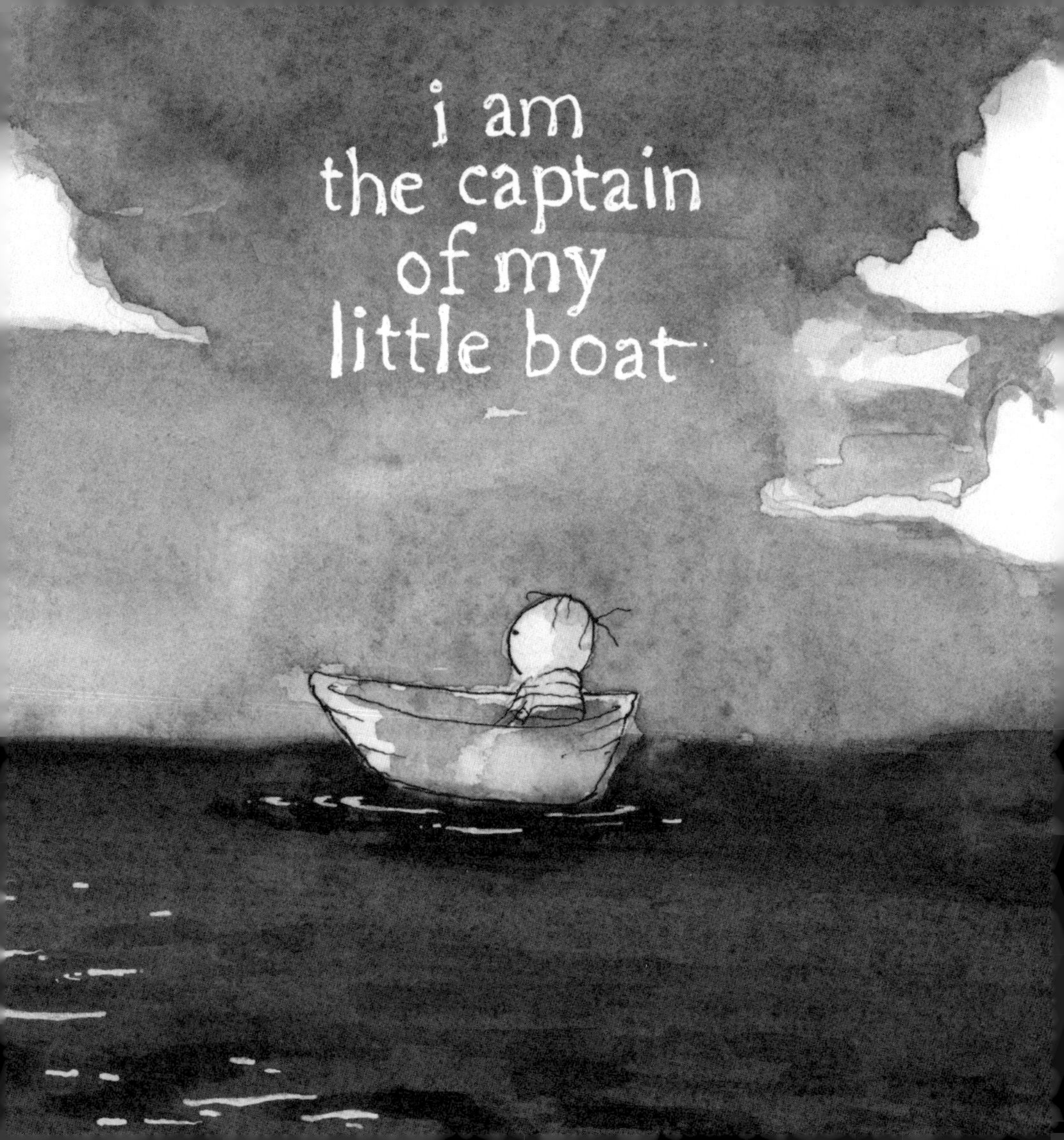
i am
the captain
of my
little boat

Gratitude List

Amber

Mom and Dad

Grandmom Claire

Megan, peter, Ayden, and Audrey

Myrsini and Matt

Lisa and Maddie

and Everyone who reads my comics - thank you.

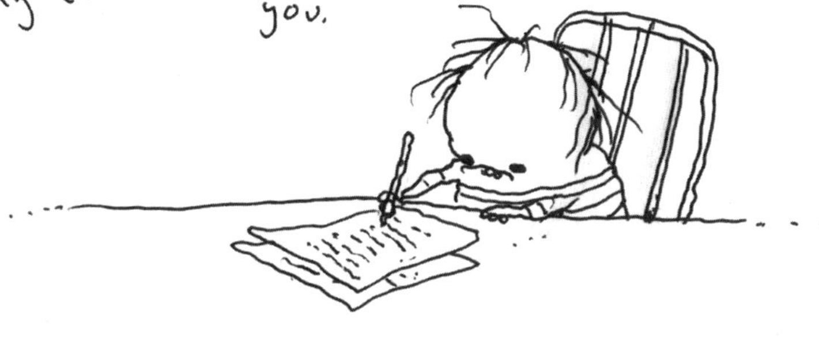

author photo

Josh Mecouch (pictured) is a cartoonist. He lives in New York City with his girlfriend and their pug, Mabel.

He is allergic to dairy.